GUIDANCE
FOR THE GOURMET

23 "RECIPES" TO TEACH CHILDREN LIFESKILL LESSONS

By Wanda S. Cook, M.Ed.

ABOUT THE AUTHOR

Wanda S. Cook has a B.S. in Education, an M.Ed in guidance and counseling, and is currently pursuing certification as a licensed professional counselor. She has been an elementary counselor for 11 years at Francis Elementary and currently serves as the sixth-grade counselor for Reed Academy, a fifth and sixth grade magnet school in the Aldine Independent School District in Houston, Texas. Mrs. Cook has presented workshops for teachers, counselors, and administrators.

Mrs. Cook is married to Joseph, friend and husband, and is the mother of two wonderful sons.

A native Floridian, she has resided in Texas for the past 25 years.

GUIDANCE FOR THE GOURMET

10-DIGIT ISBN: 1-57543-142-4   13-DIGIT ISBN: 978-1-57543-142-0

COPYRIGHT © 2006 MAR*CO PRODUCTS, INC.
Published by mar*co products, inc.
1443 Old York Road
Warminster, PA 18974
1-800-448-2197
www.marcoproducts.com

GRAPHIC DESIGN: Cameon Funk

TABLE OF CONTENTS

SECTION 1: LIFE SKILLS 7

MARVELOUS, MAGNIFICENT ME! 9

GUIDANCE FOR THE GOURMET MEAL #1
BULLYING: SHONDRA, CLASS BULLY 10
   APPETIZER: BOWLING FOR BULLIES ROLL-UPS 10
   MAIN COURSE: MENACING MINIATURE MEATLOAF 11
   DESSERT: MEAN-TO-MELLOW THANK-YOU TORTES 15
      THANK-YOU CARD 16

GUIDANCE FOR THE GOURMET MEAL #2
BEHAVIOR: KATE KATHERINE KOTTER DOESN'T LIKE THE WORD ... NO! 17
   APPETIZER: "YES/NO" SPICY SCRAMBLES 17
   MAIN COURSE: HAVE IT MY WAY MACARONI 18
   DESSERT: "TRUCE TREE" TRUFFLES 21
      REQUEST CARDS 22
      ANSWER CARDS 24
      DIAGRAM OF TREE CONSTRUCTION 26
      FRUIT PATTERNS 27

GUIDANCE FOR THE GOURMET MEAL #3
GOSSIP: STOP MAKING TROUBLE, ELIZABETH KAYE 33
   APPETIZER: GOSSIPING GARLIC SPREAD 33
   MAIN COURSE: BUSYBODY BEEF BURRITOS 34
   DESSERT: TRUE FRIEND FRITTERS 36

GUIDANCE FOR THE GOURMET MEAL #4
ACCEPTING BLAME: A LITTLE BUG DID IT 37
   APPETIZER: MISCHIEVOUS MELON BALLS 37
   MAIN COURSE: DASTARDLY DO-RIGHT DUMPLINGS 38
   DESSERT: IMAGINARY BUG SORBET 40

GUIDANCE FOR THE GOURMET MEAL #5
WORRYING: WHY I WORRY 41
   APPETIZER: WORRY-FREE HOPSCOTCH WAFERS 41
   MAIN COURSE: NO PROBLEM PORK PATTIES 42
   DESSERT: BE HAPPY CATERPILLAR CRUNCHIES 44
      WORRY-FREE WAFERS 45
      WORRY GRID 46

GUIDANCE FOR THE GOURMET MEAL #6
SELF-CONFIDENCE: "NO ONE WILL LIKE ME," CRIED MAGGIE MCGEE 47
   APPETIZER: SELF-ESTEEM MUSIC MELTS 47
   MAIN COURSE: SEEKING SELF-LOVE SUBS 48
   DESSERT: SWEET AND SILKY SELF-ESTEEM SILHOUETTES 51
      BOY SILHOUETTE 52
      GIRL SILHOUETTE 53

GUIDANCE FOR THE GOURMET MEAL #7
THE IMPORTANCE OF RULES: THE SCHOOL WITHOUT RULES 54
   APPETIZER: FAMOUS SWITCH-A-ROO AMBROSIA 54
   MAIN COURSE: CHAOTIC CHICKEN CHOWDER 55
   DESSERT: SCHOOL RULES SCOOPS 58
      ICE CREAM CONE 59
      SCOOPS 60

GUIDANCE FOR THE GOURMET MEAL #8
PERFECTION: PRUDENCE PRIMROSE PICKENHEIMER 61
   APPETIZER: PERFECT POTATO PUSH 61
   MAIN COURSE: PRECISE AND POLITE POT PIE 62
   DESSERT: SUGARLESS NO-STRESS STRING ART 64
      BOWS 65
      BOW TIES 66

GUIDANCE FOR THE GOURMET MEAL #9
BEHAVIOR: JACK TALKS BACK **67**
   APPETIZER: ORNERY HAM SCRAMBLES 67
   MAIN COURSE: OH-SO-SASSY SALMON SURPRISE 68
   DESSERT: POLITE PIE STREAMERS 71
      RESPECTFUL RULES 72

GUIDANCE FOR THE GOURMET MEAL #10
TATTLING: NORMA-NELL, TATTLETALE **83**
   APPETIZER: TATTLE OR TELL CHEDDAR TALES 83
   MAIN COURSE: TATTLE-TATTLE TELL ALL TORTELLINI 84
   DESSERT: NO TATTLING BOOKMARK BEAUTIES 87
      TATTLING OR TELLING STRIPS 88
      BOOKMARKS 90

GUIDANCE FOR THE GOURMET MEAL #11
BEING HOME ALONE: IF YOU'RE HOME ALONE **91**
   APPETIZER: FAITHFUL FRUIT FLOATIES 91
   MAIN COURSE: SAFE AND SECURE SAVORY STEW 92
   DESSERT: EMERGENCY PLAN PUDDING 95
      IF YOU'RE HOME ALONE SITUATION/ACTION STRIPS 96
      MY EMERGENCY PLAN 98

GUIDANCE FOR THE GOURMET MEAL #12
ACCEPTING OTHERS: THE PINK SPOOKY MEN **102**
   APPETIZER: SPOOKY MAN SOUFFLE TOSS 102
   MAIN COURSE: FEARLESS FLOUNDER FILLETS 103
   DESSERT: MARSHMALLOW MASK MARMALADE 107

GUIDANCE FOR THE GOURMET MEAL #13
PROPER DIET: EAT YOUR BROCCOLI, IRENE **108**
   APPETIZER: FINICKY MINI-MORSELS 108
   MAIN COURSE: JIFFY NO-JUNK JAMBALAYA 109
   DESSERT: WHOLESOME HONEY TREATS 113
      FOOD STRIPS 114

GUIDANCE FOR THE GOURMET MEAL #14
EXPRESSING DIFFERENCES: MALCOLM AND THE PURPLE TIE **118**
   APPETIZER: OPPOSITIONAL ORANGE SQUARES 118
   MAIN COURSE: "AGREE WITH ME" QUICHE-A-LA-KING 119
   DESSERT: DUELING DIFFERENCES DRAMA BARS 122
      DUELING DRAMA SITUATION SHEET 123

GUIDANCE FOR THE GOURMET MEAL #15
UNHEALTHY FOOD CHOICES: THE MUGAROTS **124**
   APPETIZER: TEMPTING TREASURE TREATS 124
   MAIN COURSE: GREEN AND GROOVY GARDEN GOULASH 125
   DESSERT: HELEN'S HEALTH FRUIT SQUARES 130
      DIRECTIVE CARDS 131

GUIDANCE FOR THE GOURMET MEAL #16
JEALOUSY: THE SAPLING **132**
   APPETIZER: JEALOUS JUBILEE 132
   MAIN COURSE: ENVY-FREE EGG FRITTERS 133
   DESSERT: JEALOUS GELATIN JINGLES 136
      MUSICAL STRIPS 137

GUIDANCE FOR THE GOURMET MEAL #17
ANGER: MAD GEORGE **138**
   APPETIZER: HOPPIN' MAD MUFFINS 138
   MAIN COURSE: FURIOUSLY FLAMING FISH FLORENTINE 139
   DESSERT: DELECTABLE MAD-BUSTER SCROLLS 141
      MAD-BUSTERS 146

GUIDANCE FOR THE GOURMET MEAL #18
ORGANIZATION/TIDINESS: JOEY AND HIS BIG MESS **147**
    APPETIZER: CLEAN UP CHOWDER 147
    MAIN COURSE: TERRIFIC TIDY-UP TACOS 148
    DESSERT: ORGANIZED BOX CAKE 151
        RED GROUP CARDS 152
        BLUE GROUP CARDS 161

GUIDANCE FOR THE GOURMET MEAL #19
PERSONAL HYGIENE: HUDSON HAROLDSON'S HAIR **163**
    APPETIZER: CLEAN-SWEEP APPLE BUTTER 163
    MAIN COURSE: SPOTLESS SPINACH SOUP 164
    DESSERT: HYGIENE BASKET TURNOVERS 166

SECTION 2: COPING SKILLS 167

WHEN LIFE SERVES UP BITTER GREENS **168**

GUIDANCE FOR THE GOURMET MEAL #20
DEPRESSION: JOHN-MICHAEL'S EYES **169**
    WILTED NO-WEEP WATERCRESS TOSS 169
        PUT THE GREENS IN THE BOWL (FACING THE ISSUE) 169
        ADD FRUITS AND SPICES (UNDERSTANDING EMOTIONS) 172
        REMOVE THE TOUGH STEMS (INFORMATION AND FACTS) 173
        DRIZZLE WITH DRESSING (COPING STRATEGIES) 174
        TOSS AND EAT (THERAPEUTIC ACTIVITIES) 175
            HOW ARE YOU FEELING TODAY? 176
            WHAT IS DEPRESSION? 177
            WORDFIND 178

GUIDANCE FOR THE GOURMET MEAL #21
GRIEF AND LOSS: ABBY'S LULLABY **179**
    SORROWFUL SORREL SALAD 179
        PUT THE GREENS IN THE BOWL (FACING THE ISSUE) 179
        ADD FRUITS AND SPICES (UNDERSTANDING EMOTIONS) 186
        REMOVE THE TOUGH STEMS (INFORMATION AND FACTS) 187
        DRIZZLE WITH DRESSING (COPING STRATEGIES) 188
        TOSS AND EAT (THERAPEUTIC ACTIVITIES) 189
            FEELINGS 190
            LIFE AND DEATH 191
            WHAT TO DO ABOUT MY FEELINGS 192

GUIDANCE FOR THE GOURMET MEAL #22
GRIEF AND LOSS: AFTER GRANDPA WENT AWAY **193**
    SORROWFUL SORREL SALAD 193
        PUT THE GREENS IN THE BOWL (FACING THE ISSUE) 193
        ADD FRUITS AND SPICES (UNDERSTANDING EMOTIONS) 195
        REMOVE THE TOUGH STEMS (INFORMATION AND FACTS) 196
        DRIZZLE WITH DRESSING (COPING STRATEGIES) 197
        TOSS AND EAT (THERAPEUTIC ACTIVITIES) 198
            EXTRA!! SPECIAL CONDIMENTS FOR SORROWFUL SORREL 199

GUIDANCE FOR THE GOURMET MEAL #23
UNSAFE LIVING CONDITIONS: YOHAWNI'S BACKYARD **200**
    ANXIOUS ARUGULA SALAD 200
        PUT THE GREENS IN THE BOWL (FACING THE ISSUE) 200
        ADD FRUITS AND SPICES (UNDERSTANDING EMOTIONS) 203
        REMOVE THE TOUGH STEMS (INFORMATION AND FACTS) 204
        DRIZZLE WITH DRESSING (COPING STRATEGIES) 205
        TOSS AND EAT (THERAPEUTIC ACTIVITIES) 206
            MY PERFECT NEIGHBORHOOD 207
            DO YOU KNOW WHAT TO DO? 208

SECTION I
LIFE SKILLS

MARVELOUS, MAGNIFICENT ME!

By Wanda S. Cook

I'm simply marvelous!
Can't you see?
I love every special
part of me.

My hands, my eyes,
the way I speak.
My smile, my style,
I am unique.

I can fly to the sky.
I can roar like the sea.
I can ride the wind.
Because I am me!

I can be whatever
I want to be.
You can, too,
if you believe!

I'm strong, I'm smart,
as cool as can be.
And I'm proud to be
marvelous, magnificent me!

SHONDRA, CLASS BULLY

APPETIZER

BOWLING FOR BULLIES ROLL-UPS

Appetizer Ingredients:

Master Chef:
☐ Tennis ball

Student Chefs (5 -10 players):
☐ Small plastic drink bottle for each player
☐ Sticky label
☐ Pencil or marker

Appetizer Preparation:

Remove labels from the bottles or have the children do so at the beginning of the lesson. If you have a small number of players, you may wish to add extra bottles without names. Decide what pattern you wish to use to line up the bottles. For example: like 10 pins in a bowling alley, in a straight line, etc.

Appetizer Activity:

Give each student a small plastic bottle, a sticky label, and a pencil or marker. Then say:

After you write your name on the label and stick it to the bottle, I will line the bottles up in a row *(or whatever pattern you choose)*. You will then take turns rolling the tennis ball and trying to topple the bottles. When a bottle is toppled, the person whose name is on that bottle must tell about a time when he or she was bullied or saw someone else being bullied. I will then remove the bottle that has been toppled. The game will end when all of the bottles have been toppled and each child has shared a story.

MENACING MINIATURE MEATLOAF

Main Course Ingredients:

Master Chef:
- ☐ *Shondra, Class Bully* story (pages 11-14)
- ☐ Chalkboard and colored chalk

Student Chefs:
- ✗ No materials required

Main Course Preparation:

None required.

Main Course Activity:

BEGIN by asking the children: "What is a bully?" *(Pause for responses.)*

Read the following story aloud to the children. Pause at the involvement questions for the children's answers.

Shondra, Class Bully

The Eagle Heights bus, route 243,
bounced up to the schoolyard gate.
Each morning, it arrived quite early,
but today it was noisy and late!

As the tires slid
to a screeching halt,
children cried out,
"It wasn't our fault!

"We did what you asked.
Believe us, it's true!"
Their teeth seemed to chatter
and their nails they did chew.

STOP Ask the children: "What do you think will happen next?"

"We gave you our money,
our homework, our toys,
and our Super Speed bikes,"
said two red-headed boys.

"I sloshed in the rain
when you took my umbrella,
then dried your wet boots,"
said a trembling Stella.

"So please don't be mad.
No one told us," said Kelli,
"to serve your hot breakfast
with a squeeze of chilled jelly."

Then I witnessed
a most terrible sight:
Someone on that bus
was starting a fight!

First, papers were ripped,
then backpacks and books.
Such kicking and punching,
the whole bus shook!

The children were frightened.
They started to yell.
Then a **BIG** voice said deeply,
"You better not tell!"

STOP Ask the children: "How did the children feel? How would you have felt?"

The boom of that voice
caused the schoolyard to quake.
To tattle, the children,
knew would be a mistake.

So they stood there in silence
and said not a word,
shivering and shaking
from that voice they'd just heard.

Then they marched off the bus
as though in a trance,
led by their driver,
Senor Pepe McVance.

Eyes fixed, they stared,
still no sounds to be heard.
The whole situation
seemed very absurd.

STOP Have a few children demonstrate how the students looked as they marched off the bus.

Then off jumped Shondra,
the new girl in town.
She wore ribbons and pigtails
and a serious frown.

STOP Have two or three children come to the board and draw a picture of Shondra.

She glared at the children,
nodded, then spat.
"That means we can leave,"
whispered Ashley to Matt.

"Dismissed!" she confirmed,
and they dashed into school.
Shondra picked up her purse
and strolled in, real cool.

"Good morning, Ms. Kwan!"
she yelled to her teacher.
"Good morning, sweet Shondra,
you wonderful creature."

"Sweet?" whispered Seth
from the back of the room.
"Try Shondra, Class Bully,
Tiny Princess of Doom!"

STOP Ask the children: "How did Shondra feel about her teacher?"

This strange day continued,
and took a new twist.
During reading, I saw
Shondra scribbling a list.

When the teacher wasn't looking,
she tossed it to Sean.
"Make copies," she snarled,
"for everyone!"

Sean took Shondra's list,
couldn't believe what she'd written.
He tried giving it back,
but his finger was bitten.

STOP Ask the children: "Why did Shondra bite Sean's finger?"

The list read,
if I may quote:
"Trish, you will give me
your new red coat.

"John-Michael,
I'm taking your blue slappy pens,
Jayla's charm bracelet,
and that fine ring of Ben's.

"I'll have Caitlin's grape markers,
Blake's autographed hats,
Meg's strawberry stickers,
and Lynn's scarf with the cats.

"For lunch I will dine
on Shameka Brown's fries,
Jim's juicy pickle,
and Joe's three apple pies."

STOP Ask the children: "Why do you think Shondra wanted to take things from the children?"

"For recess,
please note and abide:
As of now, I am
Queen of the Slide.

"I alone will decide
who can and can not play
with the balls, bats,
and swings every day."

Since Shondra was new,
she thought it would be cool,
to shake the hands
of each kid at her school.

She squeezed till they squirmed,
then ordered with delight,
"When you learn to obey me,
everything will be all right."

STOP Ask the children: "Why did Shondra squeeze their hands so hard?"

When she spoke, everyone stood still.
(Though some really shook in their boots.)
And when her speech was finally done,
to Shondra they all gave salutes.

Proud that her mission was over and done,
she strolled to the Eagle Heights bus
on a red velvet carpet,
a gift from Jada and Russ.

This madness continued far too long.
The kids' nerves were badly frayed.
Trying do all that Shondra demanded,
and still keep up their good grades.

At the end of one day, Libby and Kaye
knew that they had to be brave.
So they told Ms. Kwan what Shondra had done
and how badly she behaved.

STOP Ask the children: "Have you ever been brave? Were Libby and Kaye tattling?"

The teacher listened and was not amused
by the things the girls had to say.
In fact, she was shocked that her little pupil
behaved in this horrible way.

When Shondra strolled in the very next day
and yelled, "Good morning, Ms. Kwan!"
Her teacher smiled and whispered to ask,
"My dear, may we visit at one?"

STOP Ask the children: "Did Shondra know that she had been caught?"

Shondra met with her teacher out by the slide,
and learned her secrets had all been revealed.
She threw her purse, she'd never felt worse,
stamped her feet, and started to squeal.

She rolled in the dirt, soiling her new skirt.
(The one she had taken from Kaye.)
Ms. Kwan didn't balk, but said, "Come, dear,
let's talk about what happened today."

Shondra squealed even louder,
pounding her fist on the ground.
But Ms. Kwan spoke very softly
until she finally calmed down.

"I didn't want you to know," she whimpered,
"about the horrible things that I've done."
She brushed the dirt from her pretty new skirt
and with her humble confession begun …

STOP Ask the children: "What is a *confession*?"

"I bullied other children
so they wouldn't bully me.
I've been teased, hit, and pinched
since I was age three.

"Still, what I did was
the wrong thing to do.
I hurt others, myself,
and especially you.

"I'm sorry for fighting
and other wrong things I've done.
I won't do them again,
I promise, Ms. Kwan.

"I'll give back what I took.
I'll do it today.
And never again
will I act that way."

So Shondra gave back
Trish's new red coat
and everything else
from that list that she wrote.

She gave back John-Michael
his blue slappy pens,
Jayla her bracelet,
and that fine ring of Ben's.

She gave back Caitlin's grape markers
and Blake's autographed hats.
She gave back Meg's strawberry stickers
and Lynn's scarf with the cats.

She gave the carpet back
to Jada and Russ.
(The red one she used
when she walked to the bus.)

She no longer dined on
Shameka Brown's fries,
Jim's juicy pickle,
or Joe's three apple pies.

Being kind wasn't easy.
But after a while,
that serious frown
turned into a smile.

STOP Ask the children: "How do you think Shondra is feeling now?"

Shondra felt good
at the end of that day.
So she picked up her purse
and skipped happily away.

But she didn't skip far before
she kicked and slugged Thomas.
Then she remembered Ms. Kwan,
her confession, and promise.

For weeks after that,
she still snarled once in a while,
but mainly she wore
her pretty, new smile.

In time, Shondra changed and proudly became
all that she'd promised her teacher,
moved by the way she was greeted each day,
"a dear, sweet and wonderful creature!"

FINISH the story by asking the children: "Why is Ms. Kwan so important to Shondra? Have you ever had a teacher like Ms. Kwan?"

MEAN-TO-MELLOW THANK-YOU TORTES

Dessert Ingredients:

Master Chef:
- ✗ No materials required

Student Chefs:
- ☐ Copy of *Thank-You Card* (page 16)
- ☐ Pencil
- ☐ Scissors
- ☐ Glue or tape
- ☐ Ribbon or yarn
- ☐ Any decorative items you wish to use

Dessert Preparation:

Make a copy of *Thank-You Card* for each child.

Dessert Activity:

Introduce the activity by saying:

> Ms. Kwan helped Shondra change from mean to mellow. Shondra wanted to give the teacher something special for believing in her, so she made a fancy thank-you note. Make a thank-you note for someone who has helped you do the right thing. Decorate it and tie a beautiful ribbon or yarn around it when you finish. Make it look delicious!

Distribute the *Thank-You Card* sheet, scissors, pencil, glue or tape, ribbon or yarn, and any other decorative items you have chosen for the children. When the children have finished writing the thank-you notes, instruct them to fold and glue them according to the directions. Then have them share their notes with the group. Encourage the children to give their thank-you notes to the people to whom they are written.

THANK-YOU CARD

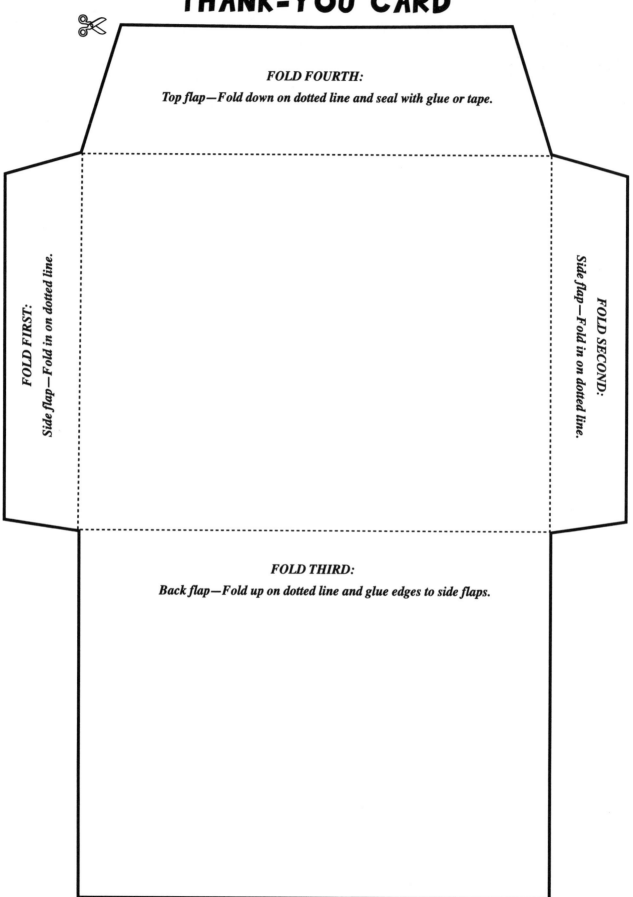

FOLD FOURTH:

Top flap—Fold down on dotted line and seal with glue or tape.

FOLD FIRST:

Side flap—Fold in on dotted line.

FOLD SECOND:

Side flap—Fold in on dotted line.

FOLD THIRD:

Back flap—Fold up on dotted line and glue edges to side flaps.

KATE KATHERINE KOTTER DOESN'T LIKE THE WORD ... NO!

APPETIZER

"YES/NO" SPICY SCRAMBLES

Appetizer Ingredients:

Master Chef:
- ☐ Copy of *Request Cards* (pages 22-23)
- ☐ Copy of *Answer Cards* (pages 24-25)
- ☐ Blue and yellow card stock

Student Chefs (4 or more players):
- ✗ No materials required

Appetizer Preparation:

Reproduce the *Answer Cards* on blue card stock and the *Request Cards* on yellow card stock. Then cut the cards apart. You may use the blank cards to write other relevant situations.

Appetizer Activity:

Deal one card to each child. Be sure to deal out an equal number of *Answer Cards* and *Request Cards.* Then say:

Each of you has a card. Some cards are blue and others are yellow. If you have a blue card, you have an *Answer Card.* If you have a yellow card, you have a *Request Card.* The *Request Cards* are labeled with questions kids ask their parents or other adults. On my cue, those of you with *Request Cards* are to go around the room and find a person whose *Answer Card* has the correct word to answer your request. When you find that person, you must both agree that the answer is correct. After everyone has paired up, you will share your request and answer with our group.

May I skip school and go to the movies?

GUIDANCE FOR THE GOURMET REQUEST
© 2006 MAR*CO PRODUCTS, INC. 1-800-4

NO

GUIDANCE FOR THE GOURMET REQUEST CARDS
© 2006 MAR*CO PRODUCTS, INC. 1-800-448-2197

HAVE IT MY WAY MACARONI

Main Course Ingredients:

Master Chef:
- ☐ Chalkboard and chalk
- ☐ *Kate Katherine Kotter Doesn't Like The Word … No* story (pages 18-20)

Student Chefs:
- ✗ No materials required

Main Course Preparation:

None required.

Main Course Activity:

Read the following story aloud to the children. Pause at the involvement questions for the children's answers.

Kate Katherine Kotter
Doesn't Like The Word … No

Kate Katherine Kotter
doesn't like the word "no."
So her mother said "yes"
to her every request!

"**Yes**, dear, you may
eat ice cream and cake
instead of the dinner
I worked all day to make.

"And **yes**, you may dress
in your new coat and shoes
to slop in the mud
or whatever you choose.

"And **yes**, I will do
each one of your chores
while you crayon the ceiling,
the walls, and the floors.

"And **yes**, it's OK
to dump paint in your bed,
stick gum to the sofa,
even shave my head!"

STOP Ask the children: "Does Kate like to have her own way?"

"And **yes**, **yes**, of course
I will buy you a horse.
An octopus, too,
if that's what I must do."

STOP Ask the children: "Would your mom say *yes* if you asked for a pet octopus?"

"**Yes**, **yes**, stay awake
until three in the morn
to bang on your drums
And toot your loud horn.

"Play toss? **Yes**, you may
with my favorite fine dishes.
And **yes**, **yes**, three times **yes**
to your 300 wishes!"

STOP Ask the children: "Why do you think Kate's mom said *yes* to so many ridiculous things?"

Saying "yes" all the time
nearly drove her mom crazy.
"You need a vacation,"
said her friend, Dr. Daisy.

So Mother sailed out
and Aunt Edna flew in.
Kate Katherine's world
was set for a spin!

"Aunt Edna," said Kate,
"we have things to discuss.
Now listen politely,
so there won't be a fuss."

Kate then told her aunt
she'd eat ice cream and cake,
instead of the dinner
she worked all day to make.

And that she would dress
in her new coat and shoes
to slop in the mud
or whatever she'd choose.

And that she would dump
paint in her bed,
stick gum to the sofa,
and shave Auntie's gray head.

STOP Ask the children: "What do you think
will happen next?"

"**No**," said Aunt Edna,
"that simply won't be.
Kate Katherine Kotter,
no **yeses** from me."

Kate stood there befuddled.
Her jaw dropped to the ground.
Then her cute, tiny face
made one big, ugly frown.

Her eyes narrowed darkly,
then out came this roar,
so loud and so big
it blew out the door!

Then like a strong whirlwind,
she ripped up the room.
Her aunt smiled and thought,
"She will calm herself soon."

Kate huffed and she puffed
when her tantrum was done.
She was proud of herself,
'cause she thought she'd won.

STOP Ask the children: "Why did Kate have
such a tantrum?"

She spoke to Aunt Edna,
breathing deeply and low.
"Didn't anyone tell you?
I hate the word **no**!"

"Your mother did tell me,
right here in this letter.
But, my **no's** will not change,
now hang up your sweater."

Too tired to fight back,
Kate washed up for dinner.
But she thought while she ate,
"I will be the winner!"

The next day made Kate
more determined to win
back all her **yeses**,
and freedom again.

"Aunt Edna," she said slowly,
"let's do this once more.
I crayon the ceiling,
I do not do chores."

STOP Ask the children: "Was Kate Katherine
stubborn? How do you know?"

"I will stay awake
until three in the morn,
to bang on my drums
and toot my loud horn.

"And **yes, yes**, of course
you will buy me a horse.
An octopus, too,
that's what you must do."

"**No**!" said Aunt Edna.
"No **yeses** from me.
While Mom is away,
this is how it will be!"

Kate stood there befuddled.
Her jaw dropped to the ground.
Then her cute, tiny face
made one big, ugly frown.

Her eyes narrowed darkly,
then out came this roar,
so loud and so big
it blew out the door!

Then like a strong whirlwind,
she ripped up the room.
Her aunt smiled and thought,
"She will calm herself soon."

Kate huffed and she puffed
when her tantrum was done.
She was proud of herself,
'cause she thought she'd won.

She spoke to Aunt Edna,
breathing deeply and low.
"Didn't anyone tell you?
I hate the word **no**!"

STOP Ask the children: "What do you think Aunt Edna will do now?"

Aunt Edna said calmly,
"My **no's** will not change.
And we'll no longer play
this ridiculous game.

"It's high time you learn
that you cannot win
by shouting and pouting
again and again."

"But I suppose," said Aunt Edna,
"that I would say **yes**,
to more sensible things
you'd care to request."

So Kate Katherine agreed
to be calm and polite,
and she earned a few **yeses**
and ice cream that night.

Soon after their truce,
Kate's mother returned.
Mom was proud of her Kate
and the lesson she'd learned.

Now, Mom, Kate, and Auntie
vacation together.
Accepting the **no's**
Has made life so much better!

FINISH the story by asking the children to name some ways that Kate's behavior changed after Aunt Edna's visit. (Write the children's answers on the board—no pouting, no temper tantrums, no shouting, no ripping up the room, accepting *no's*.)

"TRUCE TREE" TRUFFLES

Dessert Ingredients:

Master Chef:
- ☐ Scissors
- ☐ Green construction paper
- ☐ Ruler
- ☐ Red, orange, purple, light green, pink, and yellow construction paper
- ☐ *Diagram Of Tree Construction* (page 26)
- ☐ Fruit (pages 27-32)

Student Chefs:
- ☐ Scissors
- ☐ 12" x 18" green construction paper
- ☐ Ruler
- ☐ Gluestick
- ☐ Tape
- ☐ Pencil

Dessert Preparation:

Reproduce enough fruit, using the appropriate construction paper colors, so each child may have one piece of fruit for each of the behaviors Kate Katherine changed.

Dessert Activity:

Introduce the activity by saying:

> Kate Katherine and Aunt Edna made a truce. Today each of you is going to make a 3-D *Truce Tree*.

Distribute a piece of 12" x 18" green construction paper, scissors, a gluestick, a pencil, tape, and a ruler to each student. (**Note:** See diagram on page 26.) While demonstrating, say:

> Fold the green construction paper lengthwise. Cut the paper in half on the fold. Put the two pieces of paper together and fold them lengthwise again. Take your pencil and draw half of a tree on the side of the paper with the fold. Be sure to make the trunk large. Cut both pieces of paper out on the lines you have drawn for the tree. You now have two trees that are exactly the same. Take your ruler and draw a horizontal line on the fold halfway up the trunk of one tree. Then take your ruler and draw a line on the fold halfway down from the top of the other tree. For example, if your tree is 12 inches long, draw a line six inches from the top of the tree. Start from the top of one tree and cut a slit on the fold, to the halfway line. On the other tree, start from the bottom and cut a slit on the fold to the halfway line. Slide the trees together through the slits. If necessary, hold them together with tape. Your tree should now stand on its own.

> I want you to choose the kinds of fruit you would like on your tree. You may have one kind or many kinds of fruit, but you must have one piece of fruit for each thing Kate Katherine agreed to do.

Review the things written on the board that Kate Katherine agreed to do. Show the children the fruit choices. Then say:

> Select one piece of fruit for each of Kate Katherine's new behaviors. Cut out the fruit and write the behavior on it. Then glue your fruit to your tree. When you have finished, you may share your trees with the group.

May I spend the night with a friend?

May I skip school and go to the movies?

May I skip showering for a week?

May I do my homework after dinner?

May the dog sleep in my bed?

May I throw my muddy boots on the sofa?

May I have a hotdog for dinner?

May I ride on the motorcycle with my new classmate's big brother?

May I ride my bike if I put on my helmet?

May I bring 15 friends over for dinner tonight?

May I have a soft drink just for tonight?

GUIDANCE FOR THE GOURMET REQUEST CARDS
© 2006 MAR∗CO PRODUCTS, INC. 1-800-448-2197

May I go online to find the answers to my homework assignment?

GUIDANCE FOR THE GOURMET REQUEST CARDS
© 2006 MAR∗CO PRODUCTS, INC. 1-800-448-2197

GUIDANCE FOR THE GOURMET REQUEST CARDS
© 2006 MAR∗CO PRODUCTS, INC. 1-800-448-2197

GUIDANCE FOR THE GOURMET REQUEST CARDS
© 2006 MAR∗CO PRODUCTS, INC. 1-800-448-2197

GUIDANCE FOR THE GOURMET REQUEST CARDS
© 2006 MAR∗CO PRODUCTS, INC. 1-800-448-2197

GUIDANCE FOR THE GOURMET REQUEST CARDS
© 2006 MAR∗CO PRODUCTS, INC. 1-800-448-2197

GUIDANCE FOR THE GOURMET REQUEST CARDS
© 2006 MAR∗CO PRODUCTS, INC. 1-800-448-2197

GUIDANCE FOR THE GOURMET REQUEST CARDS
© 2006 MAR∗CO PRODUCTS, INC. 1-800-448-2197

GUIDANCE FOR THE GOURMET REQUEST CARDS
© 2006 MAR∗CO PRODUCTS, INC. 1-800-448-2197

GUIDANCE FOR THE GOURMET REQUEST CARDS
© 2006 MAR∗CO PRODUCTS, INC. 1-800-448-2197

YES

YES

YES

YES

YES

YES

NO

NO

NO

NO

NO

NO

NO

NO

MAYBE

MAYBE

MAYBE

MAYBE

MAYBE

MAYBE

DIAGRAM OF TREE CONSTRUCTION

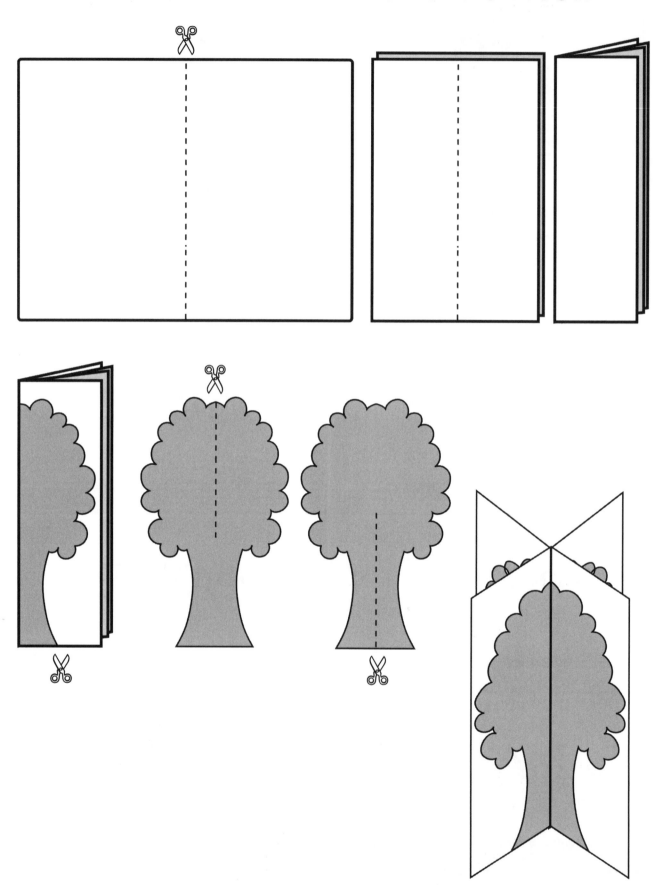

ORANGE

APPLE

PLUM

LEMON

PEAR

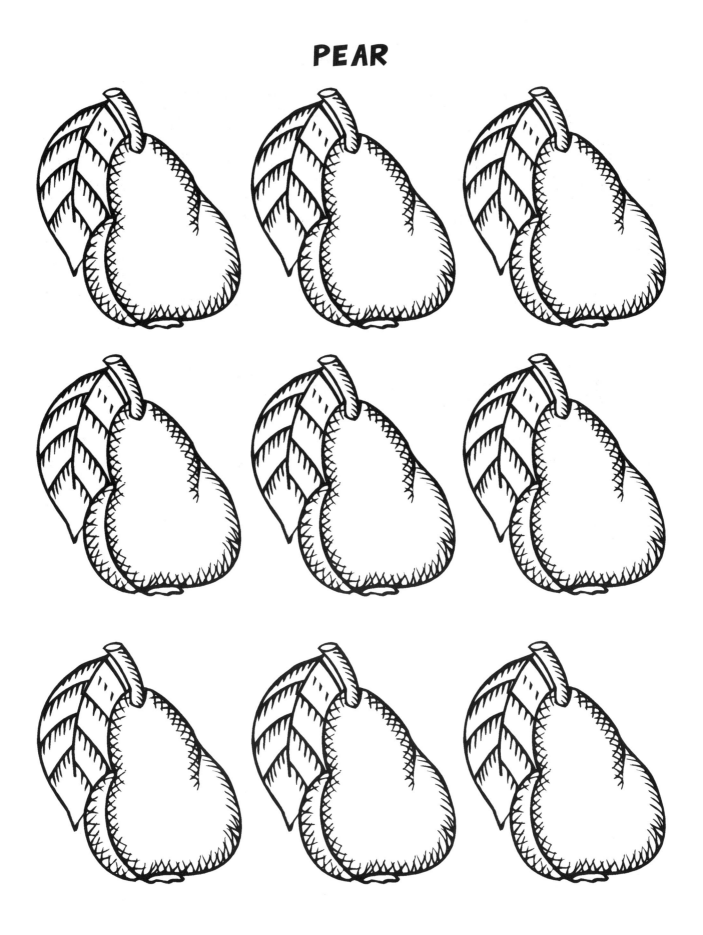

PEACH

STOP MAKING TROUBLE, ELIZABETH KAYE

APPETIZER

GOSSIPING GARLIC SPREAD

Appetizer Ingredients:

Master Chef:
  ✗ No materials required

Student Chefs: (Large groups of 10 or more children)
  ✗ No materials required

Appetizer Preparation:

Have in mind some phrases or tongue twisters to give the leaders of each group.

Appetizer Activity:

Divide the students evenly into two groups. Position them in a line or in a circle and designate a leader for each group. Then say:

> I will whisper something to the leader of each group. I will not repeat what I say. When I give the signal, each leader will whisper what I said to the next person in the group. This will continue until the message reaches the last person. If the last person can repeat the original phrase, his or her team scores a point. If one team whispers too loudly, that team will automatically be disqualified from that round. The point will go to the other team.

(**Note:** If there is an uneven number of children, the extra child may take the place of the teacher and be the person who whispers to the leader of each group.)

Tell the children how much time they have to complete the activity. When the allotted time has elapsed, the team with the most points wins the game.

BUSYBODY BEEF BURRITOS

Main Course Ingredients:

Master Chef:
☐ *Stop Making Trouble, Elizabeth Kaye*
story (pages 34-35)

Student Chefs:
✗ No materials required

Main Course Preparation:

None required.

Main Course Activity:

Read the following story aloud to the children. Pause at the involvement questions for the children's answers.

Stop Making Trouble, Elizabeth Kaye

This girl in our class
named Elizabeth Kaye
starts messy trouble
every single day.

She did it this morning:
Told my best friend, named Anna,
that I said her nose
looked like a banana.

Then she told Lauren
that Allison Brown
told Edward to pinch her
and then push her down.

James heard her tell
Ike, Jake, and Tom

that Patrick said mean things
about all of their moms.

Couldn't believe she told Cody
Luke called him a *weiner*.
And that wasn't true!
Could she be any meaner?

STOP Ask the children: "What seems to be the problem with Elizabeth Kaye?"

"Stop it," we yelled
to Elizabeth Kaye.
"No one believes
one word that you say.

"Why must you make trouble
saying things that aren't true?
How would you like it
if someone did that to you?"

"Fine," she muttered.
"Believe what you wish.
But this stuff really happened,
you can even ask Trish."

STOP Ask the children: "Did Elizabeth Kaye listen to her friends?"

"Enough is enough,"
said Marcus and Ben.
"Stop it right now,
or you'll lose every friend."

STOP Ask the children: "How do Elizabeth Kaye's friends feel about her gossiping?"

But nothing could stop her.
She whispered to Kirk,
that Evan and Bubba
called him a *jerk*.

Then Jade, she said,
told Sasha and Molly
not to be friends
with Tamika or Polly.

"Stop it," we yelled
to Elizabeth Kaye.
"No one believes
one word that you say.

"Why must you make trouble
saying things that aren't true?
How would you like it
if someone did that to you?"

But stop she did not.
She told Shannon that Willie
called her a *nerd*
and said her new glasses were silly.

She even told Stevie
that Mary and Kim
called him a bad name
on the way out to gym.

She told poor Julia
that Johnny McNair
said that he hated
her long, creepy hair.

STOP Ask the children: "Why do you think Elizabeth Kaye caused so much trouble?"

"Stop it," we yelled
to Elizabeth Kaye.
"No one believes
one word that you say.

"Why must you make trouble
saying things that aren't true?
How would you like it
if someone did that to you?"

We said this
over and over and over again.
Then one day she heard us!
At last it sunk in.

"I wasn't trying," she sniffled,
(after crying just a tad)
"to be mean to anyone
and make you all so mad."

"But still you did it.
Admit you were mean.
But why did you do it?"
questioned Lily and Jean.

"I was real bored!"
she snapped right away.
"So I did it for fun!
There, I said it, OK?"

STOP Ask the children: "Why did Elizabeth Kaye start trouble?"

"But I'll do it no more.
This mess will all end,
'cause fun is not fun,
when it's hurting a friend."

STOP Ask the children: "How is Elizabeth Kaye hurting her friends?"

So she stopped making trouble
and made up with her friends.
Everyone was delighted and
seemed happy again.

Now they spend time
helping a boy named Ray,
who tries to start trouble
each and every day.

FINISH the story by asking the children: "How do Elizabeth Kaye's friends feel about her now?"

TRUE FRIEND FRITTERS

Dessert Ingredients:

Master Chef:
- [ ] Posterboard
- [ ] Scissors
- [ ] Ruler
- [ ] Pencil
- [ ] Hole punch
- [ ] Yarn

Student Chefs:
- [ ] Construction paper
- [ ] Scissors
- [ ] Pencil
- [ ] Crayons or markers
- [ ] Glue
- [ ] Glitter

Dessert Preparation:

Using the ruler, draw a rectangle on the posterboard for each child. Then draw an arch on the posterboard for each child. Make the arch about the same width as the rectangle. Cut out both shapes.

Dessert Activity:

Introduce the activity by saying:

> Elizabeth Kaye realizes the value of friends. She wants to make something special to show her friends that she cares. We are going to make the same thing that Elizabeth Kaye made to show that we also know the value of friends and want to show our friends that we care about them.

Distribute construction paper, scissors, a pencil, and crayons or markers to each child. Then say:

> On the construction paper, draw pictures of your close friends who are classmates. Then cut the pictures out.

Distribute a posterboard rectangle, posterboard arch, glitter, and glue to each child. Then say:

> Glue your pictures to the rectangle. (*Pause for the children to complete this task.*) Now, using your crayons or markers, write in big letters across the top of the arch: *Friends Rock.* Add glitter to the arch. (*Pause for the children to complete this task.*) Glue the arch to the top of the rectangle.

Have each child come to you to have two holes punched on opposite sides of the arch. Take a piece of yarn and knot it in each hole. When you have done this, tell the children:

> We are going to start a *Friends' Circle.* Give your *Friends Rock* poster as a gift to one of the friends pictured. That person may keep the gift for one day. Then that person should pass the gift to another pictured friend. Continue this until everyone pictured has had an opportunity to keep the gift for a day. Then the gift should be returned to the person who created it.

Or say:

> We are going to display all of your gifts in (<u>NAME THE PLACE</u>) for everyone to see. In that way, all of the friends can enjoy the gifts at the same time.

A LITTLE BUG DID IT

APPETIZER

MISCHIEVOUS MELON BALLS

Appetizer Ingredients:

Master Chef:
- ✗ No materials required

Student Chefs: (An even number of players—4 or more)
- ✗ No materials required

Appetizer Preparation:

None required.

Appetizer Activity:

Divide the children into pairs. (**Note:** If there is an uneven number of children, the leader should pair up with the extra child.) Then say:

> Tell your partner about a time when you chose to misbehave.

Once all the partners have shared with each other, continue by saying:

> Now it is time to share with everyone what your misbehaving partner did. Each of you is to act out, for the rest of the group, what your partner told you. The other students will then try to guess what your partner told you.

The game ends when each of the participants has shared.

DASTARDLY DO-RIGHT DUMPLINGS

Main Course Ingredients:

Master Chef:
☐ *A Little Bug Did It* story (pages 38-39)

Student Chefs:
✗ No materials required

Main Course Preparation:

None required.

Main Course Activity:

Read the following story aloud to the children. Pause at the involvement questions for the children's answers.

A Little Bug Did It

"This math class is boring,"
said Josh to Fred.
Then he sailed three spitballs
at Zachary's head!

But he yelled out like always
when he got caught,
"Don't look at me!
It wasn't my fault."

STOP Ask the children: "Why do you think Josh is being so awful?"

"This little bug did it.
See, he sits in my ear
and whispers bad things
only I seem to hear."

"But no one believes me,
'cause this bug they can't see."

So when bad things happen
they blame it on me.

"Why, I was just shocked,
when that little bug said,
'Hey, Josh, let's throw spitballs
at Zachary's head.'

"But I told him, *no*
and I still get blamed.
No one believes me.
You think it's a game."

Then Josh slipped away
to plan his next deed.
"For my lucky victim,
I know just what I need."

STOP Ask the children: "What clues tell you that Josh is lying?"

So Josh hid his big snake
on teacher's soft seat.
She screamed when she saw it,
Josh thought that was neat.

But he yelled out like always
when he got caught,
"Don't look at me!
It wasn't my fault.

"That same tiny bug
thought it would be neat,
to put my pet snake
on my dear teacher's seat.

"I told him *no,*
and still I get blamed.
No one believes me.
You think it's a game."

STOP Say to the children: "Liar, liar pants on fire. Do you know anyone who lies like Josh?"

So Josh drank from the fountain,
and thought, "Wouldn't it be cool,
to rig up this fountain
to flood the whole school?"

But he yelled out like always
when he got caught,
"Don't look at me!
It wasn't my fault."

STOP Ask the children: "Would you want Josh to be a student in your class?"

The last thing Josh did
was out of this world.
He took Isaac's money
and punched the new girl!

STOP Ask the children: "What do you think will happen next?"

Josh was sent to the principal,
and boy was she mad!
What Josh had done
was awful and bad.

But he yelled out like always,
"It's not my fault.
A tiny bug did it
and he never gets caught."

"Well, you tell that bug,"
said the principal to Josh,
"if I ever catch him,
he's gonna get SQUASHED!

"And from now on, young man
you keep your nose clean
or else there will be trouble,
and you know what I mean!"

STOP Ask the children: "Did the principal believe Josh? How do you know?"

Then—just like that—
Josh's bug did disappear,

and it no longer whispered
into his ear.

He made things right
with his teacher and Zack,
befriended the new girl,
and paid Isaac back.

He mopped the school floors,
made them shiny and bright.
It felt really good
to do what was right.

STOP Ask the children: "Do you think Josh will settle down now?"

I guess Josh's bug
must have found Shay,
'cause she did something awful
the very next day.

She braided pink gum
in Zoe's long hair,
and laughed a mean laugh
while plaiting it there.

STOP Ask the children to demonstrate Shay's laugh.

But Shay yelled out,
after she got caught,
"Don't look at me!
It wasn't my fault."

Then Josh stood up,
"I have something to say.
This is important.
So listen up, Shay.

"If a tiny bug did it,
you'd better," said Josh,
"get rid of it now or
it's gonna get SQUASHED!"

FINISH the story by asking the children: "Do you think Josh was able to help Shay?"

IMAGINARY BUG SORBET

Dessert Ingredients:

Master Chef:
- ☐ Egg cartons
- ☐ Scissors
- ☐ Hole punch

Student Chefs:
- ☐ Crayons
- ☐ Pipe cleaners
- ☐ Googly eyes
- ☐ Glue

Dessert Preparation:

Cut the cups away from the egg cartons so each child will have an individual cup. Make a sample imaginary bug by following the activity directions.

Dessert Activity:

Introduce the activity by saying:

> Josh had an imaginary bug that he blamed when he did not want to take responsibility for his actions. What do you think his bug looked like? *(Pause for responses.)* What would your bug look like? *(Pause for responses.)* Each of you is going to make your very own imaginary bug. This is mine. *(Display your bug.)*

Distribute an egg-carton cup, crayons, pipe cleaners, glue, and googly eyes to each child. Then say:

> Color your egg-carton cup the color you would like your bug's body to be. Then raise your hand and I will come and punch two holes on each side of your egg-carton cup. Then you can thread the pipe cleaners through the cup to make your bug's legs. Glue on the googly eyes and anything else you wish to use to decorate your bug. Then give your bug a name.

Have the children share their completed bugs.

WHY I WORRY

APPETIZER

WORRY-FREE HOPSCOTCH WAFERS

Appetizer Ingredients:

Master Chef:
- ☐ Chalk
- ☐ Penny
- ☐ Scissors

Student Chefs: (2 or more players)
- ☐ Copy of *Worry-Free Wafers* (page 45)
- ☐ Small plastic bag

Appetizer Preparation:

Draw the hopscotch formation on the floor or concrete.

Make a copy of *Worry-Free Wafers* for each child. Cut out the wafers, then place the five paper wafers in a small plastic bag for each child.

Appetizer Activity:

Explain the game as follows:

The player says, "Worry-Free Me!" and then tosses the penny onto the first block. The player hops on one foot, past the block the penny is on, onto the other blocks. The player may land on two feet only on the double blocks. The player hops to the last block, turns around and comes back, picking up the penny before hopping onto the block where the penny was. When the player reaches the end of the blocks, he or she tosses the penny onto the second block and hops the hopscotch formation. The player's turn continues until he or she fails to toss the penny onto the correct block or the penny lands on the line. At that time, the next player takes a turn. This continues until each child has had a chance to play.

When the game is over, review what is written on each wafer. Then present each player with a small baggie containing five "worry-free" paper wafers. Explain that whenever something is worrying them, they should open the bag and do one of things suggested on the *Worry-Free Wafers.*

NO PROBLEM PORK PATTIES

Main Course Ingredients:

Master Chef:
☐ *Why I Worry* story (pages 42-43)

Student Chefs:
☐ Copy of *My Worry Grid* (page 46)
☐ Pencil or marker

Main Course Preparation:

Make a copy of *My Worry Grid* for each child.

Main Course Activity:

Distribute *My Worry Grid* and a pencil or marker to each child. Then read the following story aloud to the children. Pause at the involvement questions for the children's answers.

Why I Worry

You think about lots of things each day. You think about what to watch on TV. You think about what shoes to wear and you think about what there will be to eat for dinner.

Worrying is when you think about something over and over again, even though thinking about it makes you scared or nervous. And no matter how hard you try, you just can't get what's bothering you off your mind.

Worrying can give you a headache, a stomachache, and can even make you throw up. It can make it hard for you to think about your schoolwork or other important things.

STOP Ask the children: "What do you worry about?"

Trying to hide your worries can make them worse.

STOP Ask the children: "Who can you talk with about your feelings?"

Listen as some children, just like you, share what they worry about most. Decide if the things you worry about are some of the same things these children worry about. If they are, mark an "X" on the square on the *My Worry Grid* as we read along.

I worry about people who cannot hear, see, or walk. — EJ

I worry about my relative who is in the military. — NC

I worry about my grades and passing tests. — KP

I worry about my sister and my dad and my stepmom and my real mom. — AW

I worry about my grandmother or grandfather getting sick. — CT

I worry that my parents will get a divorce. — VR

I worry about homeless people. — DN

I worry about my country and the airplanes and the tall buildings. — JC

I worry that one of my parents will lose his/her job. — WE

I worry about being kidnapped. — ZA

I worry about the monster in my closet. — OT

I worry about my pet. — EN

I worry about losing my friends. — AS

I worry that a big bridge that crosses a river might break. — KS

I worry about earthquakes, hurricanes, floods, and tornados. — MS

I worry that my goldfish is lonely because his friend died and my mom won't buy him another one. — JB

I worry that my classmates will talk about me. — HS

I worry that a big, mean dog will bite me. — LJ

I worry about nuclear bombs and terrorist attacks. — MJ

I worry about a relative who is in jail. — JK

I worry because my relative smokes cigarettes. — BF

I worry that a bee or wasp might sting me. — HC

I worry that a mean stranger will sneak in through my window. — KB

I worry about the aliens from other planets. — LR

Have the children count the number of blocks they marked off and write that number on the provided line. Allow those who wish to share some of their worries to do so.

BE HAPPY CATERPILLAR CRUNCHIES

Dessert Ingredients:

Master Chef:
- ☐ Newspapers
- ☐ Paint
- ☐ Paint brushes
- ☐ Stapler and staples
- ☐ Scissors
- ☐ Paper
- ☐ Marker

Student Chefs:
- ☐ Egg cartons—one for each pair of children
- ☐ Pencil
- ☐ Glue
- ☐ Pipe cleaners
- ☐ String

Dessert Preparation:

Cut each egg carton so there are six connected cups. Cut the paper into enough strips so there is one for each child. Write *Be Happy* on each strip of paper. Cover a table with newspapers and place several colors of paint and paint brushes on the table for the students' use.

Make a sample caterpillar by following the activity directions.

Dessert Activity:

Distribute an egg carton, pencil, strip of paper with *Be Happy* written on it, string, glue, and pipe cleaners to each child. Then say:

Today you are going to make a caterpillar out of the egg carton I have just given you. Take your pencil and punch two tiny holes on the side of the first egg-carton cup. *(Display your completed caterpillar to show the students what you mean.)* Now come to the paint table and paint and decorate your caterpillar any way you wish. When your caterpillar is dry, insert the pipe cleaners into the holes you made. These pipe cleaners are your caterpillar's antennae. Take the strip of paper I gave you and glue it onto your caterpillar. Then staple or glue the string to the caterpiller so you can pull your caterpillar around.

Think of two people you trust to help when you are worried.

WORRY-FREE WAFERS

Stay positive.

Try to learn true information about things that worry you.

Talk about what is worrying you.

Take tiny steps to deal with big problems.

MY
WORRY GRID

I worry about people who cannot hear, see, or walk. — EJ	I worry about my relative who is in the military. — NC	I worry about my grades and passing tests. — KP	I worry about my sister and my dad and my stepmom and my real mom. — AW	I worry about my grandmother or grandfather getting sick. — CT
I worry that my parents will get a divorce. — VR	I worry about homeless people. — DN	I worry about my country and the airplanes and the tall buildings. — JC	I worry that one of my parents will lose his/her job. — WE	I worry about being kidnapped. —ZA
I worry about the monster in my closet. — OT	I worry about my pet. — EN		I worry about losing my friends. — AS	I worry that a big bridge that crosses a river might break. —KS
I worry about earthquakes, hurricanes, floods, and tornados. — MS	I worry that my goldfish is lonely because his friend died and my mom won't buy him another one. — JB	I worry that my classmates will talk about me. — HS	I worry that a big, mean dog will bite me. — LJ	I worry about nuclear bombs and terrorist attacks. —MJ
I worry about a relative who is in jail. —JK	I worry because my relative smokes cigarettes. —BF	I worry that a bee or wasp might sting me. — HC	I worry that a mean stranger will sneak in through my window. — KB	I worry about the aliens from other planets. — LR

GUIDANCE FOR THE GOURMET © 2006 MAR✶CO PRODUCTS, INC. 1-800-448-2197

"NO ONE WILL LIKE ME," CRIED MAGGIE MCGEE

APPETIZER

SELF-ESTEEM MUSIC MELTS

Appetizer Ingredients:

Master Chef:
- ☐ Sheets of paper
- ☐ Marker
- ☐ Tape
- ☐ Chairs equal to the number of players
- ☐ Cassette or CD player and music

Student Chefs: (10 or more players)
- ✗ No materials required

Appetizer Preparation:

On each of four sheets of paper, write one of the things Maggie McGee doesn't like about herself: big nose, frizzy hair, small eyes, scar on knee. The other sheets of paper are left blank. Place the chairs in a circle with the seats facing outward. Tape one sheet of paper to the back of each chair, making sure there is one chair and one sheet of paper for each player.

Appetizer Activity:

Explain the game as follows:

Today we are going to hear a story about a girl named Maggie McGee. There are four things Maggie does not like about herself. She has a scar on her knee, and she thinks she has small eyes, frizzy hair, and a big nose. Before we hear the story, we are going to play a game called *Self-Esteem Music Melts*. This game is played like *Musical Chairs*.

There is one chair in the circle for each player. On the back of each chair is a piece of paper, which you cannot see. One of the things Maggie McGee does not like about herself is written on each of the four sheets of paper. When I start the music, the players will walk around the chairs. When the music stops, each player will sit in a chair. Each player who is sitting in a chair whose paper describes something Maggie McGee does not like about herself will be out of the game. I will then remove four chairs whose pieces of paper are blank. The game will continue until only the four chairs with the pieces of paper listing what Maggie does not like about herself remain. I will then replace these four chairs. I will keep one with a feature Maggie McGee does not like about herself and three with blank pieces of paper. The game will continue as before. When the music stops, the person sitting in the chair whose piece of paper tells what Maggie McGee does not like about herself will be out of the game, and I will remove one chair with a blank sheet of paper. I will continue to do this until we have two players and two chairs, one with a blank sheet of paper and one with what Maggie McGee does not like about herself. This will be the last round. The player sitting in the chair with the blank piece of paper attached to its back when the music stops is the winner.

SEEKING SELF-LOVE SUBS

Main Course Ingredients:

Master Chef:
- ☐ *"No One Will Like Me," Cried Maggie McGee* story (pages 48-50)

Student Chefs:
- ☐ Art paper
- ☐ Crayons or markers

Main Course Preparation:

None required.

Main Course Activity:

Read the following story aloud to the children. Pause at the involvement questions for the children's answers.

"No One Will Like Me," Cried Maggie McGee

"No One will like me,"
cried Maggie McGee,
"'cause I have this horrible
scar on my knee.

"My nose is too big,
my eyes are too small,
and my hair is just gross!"
she continued to squall.

STOP Ask the children: "Why is Maggie so upset?"

"Don't be silly,"
said Mrs. McGee.

"Now hold still, dear,
while I tend to your knee.

"Your hair is just fine,
and your eyes and your nose.
Being the first day,
you're just scared, I suppose.

"You are a McGee,
you'll do just fine.
You'll have plenty of friends
in just a matter of time."

When Mom drove her to school
the very next day
Coach Handy was standing
near the west hallway.

"Good morning, Ms. McGee.
Nice seeing you again.
And this must be Maggie,"
Coach said, offering her hand.

She offered just one hand,
but Coach had four.
"Mom, look!" Maggie whispered.
Her books fell to the floor.

STOP Ask the children: "Why did Maggie drop her books?"

"It's OK, Maggie.
There's no need to fear.
By the end of the day,
everything will be clear."

So Maggie started her day,
with just one thought in mind:
"I'm a McGee,
I'll do just fine!"

First person she met
was Anna A. Whiney
Her mouth was gigantic,
though she was quite tiny.

Then, after lunch,
she met Bessie Bookreds,
whose family are known
for their extra-large heads.

Then she met Dina
in the gym near the hall.
In Dina's family,
all the ladies are bald!

"In our family," said Grace,
"girls have plenty hair.
But it grows from our chins
and flows everywhere!

"The teacher and her family
drool when they eat.
And they tiptoe, not walk
on all six of their feet!"

STOP Ask the children: "What is strange about Maggie's school?"

When the school day was over,
Miss Maggie McGee
ran home to her mom
just as fast as can be.

"Mom!" shouted Maggie,
when she rushed through the door.
"My school is just great.
I won't fret any more.

"Today I met Anna,
Bessie, AND GRACE!
In her family, a girl's hair grows
from the chin on her face!

"And in Dina's family,
there is no hair at all.
Well, at least not for girls,
who are like totally bald.

"Everyone at school
was so kind to me.
They said nothing at all
about the scar on my knee.

"Nor my hair, nor my eyes,
and not even my nose.
Being the first day and all,
I was scared, I suppose."

STOP Ask the children: "Why is Maggie so happy?"

"This school is the best,
out of all I have been!
I feel right at home, Mom.
I finally have friends.

"Still I don't understand
how they know you so well.
My teacher, Coach Handy,
even Principal O'Dell."

"Your school was my school,"
Mom said to Maggie McGee.
"Because I once worried
about the scars on my knee.

"About my hair, my nose,
and even my eyes.
Does this shock you, my dear?
You seem so surprised.

"But, I learned like you learned,
while attending that school.
When you accept who you are,
others will, too."

STOP Ask the children: "How did everyone know Mom so well?"

Later Mom and Maggie
called it a night.
So they turned off the TV
and turned out the light.

Then they climbed on the roof,
without scraping their knees
and curled up and slept
with the other McGees.

Yes, on the roof
'cause others have said
those distinguished McGee tails
cannot fit in their beds!

Distribute art paper and crayons or markers to each child and have the children draw a picture of Maggie and her family. Have the children share their completed drawings.

SWEET AND SILKY SELF-ESTEEM SILHOUETTES

Dessert Ingredients:

Master Chef:
- ☒ No materials required

Student Chefs:
- ☐ Copy of *Boy Silhouette* (page 52) for each boy
- ☐ Copy of *Girl Silhouette* (page 53) for each girl
- ☐ Scissors
- ☐ Glue
- ☐ Light-colored construction paper
- ☐ Pencil

Dessert Preparation:

Reproduce the appropriate silhouette for each child.

Dessert Activity:

Distribute the appropriate silhouette, a pencil, glue, scissors, and light-colored construction paper to each child. Then say:

Carefully cut out your silhouette, then glue it onto the light-colored construction paper. When you have finished, write five good things about yourself on the colored paper around the silhouette.

Display the *Sweet And Silky Self-Esteem Silhouettes* in the classroom. Then have the children take them home.

BOY SILHOUETTE

52

GUIDANCE FOR THE GOURMET © 2006 MAR•CO PRODUCTS, INC. 1-800-448-2197

BOY
SILHOUETTE

GUIDANCE FOR THE GOURMET © 2006 MAR∗CO PRODUCTS, INC. 1-800-448-2197

GIRL
SILHOUETTE

THE SCHOOL WITHOUT RULES

APPETIZER

FAMOUS SWITCH-A-ROO AMBROSIA

Appetizer Ingredients:

Master Chef:
✗ No materials required

Student Chefs: (2 or more players)
☐ Pencil
☐ Paper
☐ Art paper
☐ Crayons or markers

Appetizer Preparation:

None required.

Appetizer Activity:

Distribute paper and a pencil to each child and explain the game as follows:

On your paper, make a list of 10 family members and friends. *(Pause until the students have done this.)* Now decide which zoo or farm animal reminds you of each person listed. Write these on your paper. *(Pause until the students have done this.)*

Instead of saying the name of the animal, act it out, complete with sounds. As you do, the rest of the group will try to guess the name of the animal.

Distribute art paper and crayons or markers and have the children draw pictures of their new animal family in their *Switch-a-Roo Zoo*.

Have the children share their completed pictures.

CHAOTIC CHICKEN CHOWDER

Main Course Ingredients:

Master Chef:
- [ ] *The School Without Rules* story (page 55-57)

Student Chefs:
- ✗ No materials required

Main Course Preparation:

None required.

Main Course Activity:

Read the following story aloud to the children. Pause at the involvement questions for the children's answers.

The School Without Rules

"Principal Brown,"
yelled Billy Bland,
"I've just created
a sensational plan.

"And this, my kind sir,
is your lucky day,
because you'll be first
to hear what I say.

"But, before I begin,
I must truly confess
that your school, by far,
is one of the best.

"But I did have one problem
in class today,

when I had to work
before I could play."

STOP Ask the children: "What is Billy's problem?"

"My teacher said
that rule number one
is that students must work
before they can have fun.

"When I told her
that rule was silly,
I broke rule number two,"
said a frustrated Billy.

"So what I propose,
if you will, for this school
is to do away
with every school rule."

Principal Brown
slowly looked up,
and took a big gulp
from his favorite cup.

He thought for a while.
Not one word did he speak,
as he rocked back and forth
in his big, squeaky seat.

STOP Ask the children: "What do you think Principal Brown is thinking?"

He smiled, nearly chuckled
at this kid's new plan.
Then he spoke politely,
"As you wish, Mr. Bland."

STOP Ask the children: "Why did the principal agree to Billy's plan?"

"But, son, I must warn you,
things here will change.
Without school rules,
people will act strange."

Then Principal Brown announced
loud and clear,
"There'll be no school rules
for the rest of the year!"

At first there was silence,
so he said it again.
"Has he gone mad?"
whispered teacher Ms. Flynn.

The children all cheered
and shouted with glee,
"No rules means
we do as we please!"

Billy was happy,
but thought of one thing,
being first to play on
that zip-and-twist thing.

He was first in line,
but he didn't play
'cause Octopus Oscar
pushed him away.

With all eight sticky arms
that sprouted the day
Octopus Oscar announced,
"No rules to obey."

STOP Ask the children: "Why do you think Oscar grew arms?"

So Billy left to play
in the silky, white sand,
but was slapped by a pig
who had Pam Holland's hands.

"No hitting," he said.
"That is rule number three."
"No rules," she grunted.
"I do as I please."

Billy turned to leave.
Upset, I suppose,
after Chris the Crab
pinched his nose.

STOP Ask the children: "How is Billy feeling?"

When leaving, he heard
rude words and a roar
from a bear who was dressed
like Lisa LaNore.

"I'm leaving," he cried
and flung open the gate.
But he was chased by a bull
who snorted like Nate.

Billy barely escaped
to his afternoon room,
where he found his teacher
riding her broom.

"This place is a zoo.
Everyone has changed
from being polite
to being real strange."

He found Principal Brown
sipping herb tea
in a comfortable hammock
near the big oak tree.

"Principal Brown,"
said Billy Bland.
"I have created
an awful plan!

"Because of my problem
in class today
when I had to work
before I could play."

STOP Ask the children: "Why did Billy change his mind?"

"But now I see
that the problem is me,
'cause rules make school
a nice place to be.

"Rules are important,
like rule number three.
When there are no rules,
people do as they please."

Principal Brown said,
"This is your lucky day,
because you'll get to hear
what I have to say."

Then he announced
quite loud and clear,
"We WILL have rules
for the rest of the year."

It was noisy at first
so he said it once more.
The pushing stopped,
and so did the roar.

STOP Ask the children: "Do you think things will get back to normal?"

Teacher sat down
and gave up her broom,
to follow the rules
in her afternoon room.

And the bulls, crabs, and pigs
all hurried away
to find a new school
with no rules for that day!

SCHOOL RULES SCOOPS

Dessert Ingredients:

Master Chef:
- [ ] Copy of *Ice Cream Cone* (page 59)
- [ ] Copy of *Scoops* (page 60)
- [ ] Brown or tan construction paper or card stock
- [ ] Various colors of construction paper or card stock
- [ ] Scissors

Student Chefs:
- [ ] Scissors
- [ ] Gluestick
- [ ] Pencil

Dessert Activity:

Distribute a pencil, an ice cream cone, scissors, a gluestick, and three scoops to each child. Have the children cut out their cones and scoops. Then say:

On each cone, write one school rule. Then glue your scoops onto the ice cream cone for a yummy treat. When everyone has finished, you may share your rules with your family and friends.

Dessert Preparation:

Make a copy of *Ice Cream Cone* on brown or tan construction paper or cardstock, then cut the cones apart. Make enough copies so each child can have a cone. Using various colors of construction paper or cardstock to represent flavors of ice cream, make enough copies of *Scoops* so each child can choose his/her favorite flavor for his/her cone.

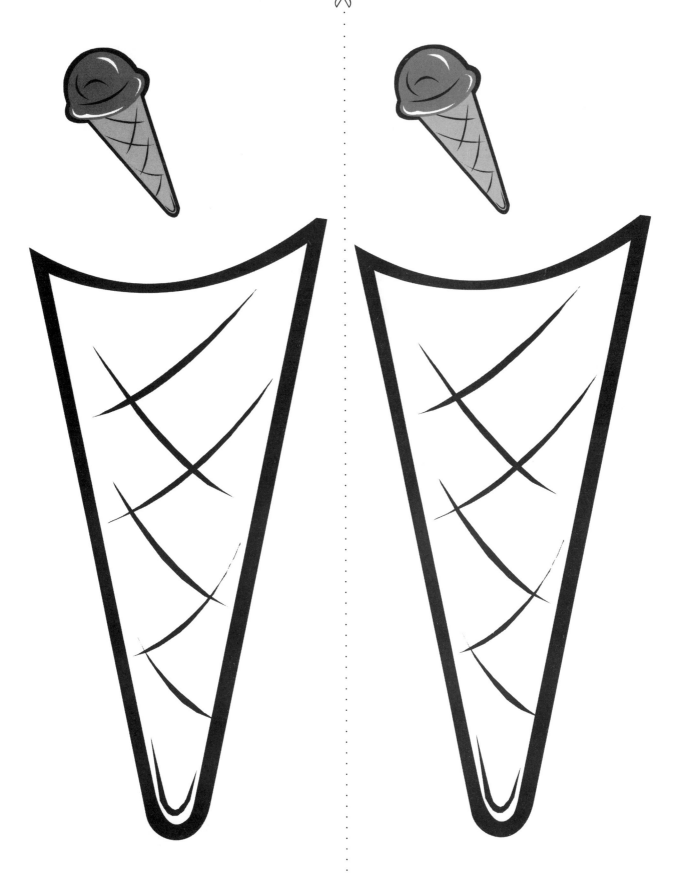

SCOOPS

GUIDANCE FOR THE GOURMET © 2006 MAR∗CO PRODUCTS, INC. 1-800-448-2197

PRUDENCE PRIMROSE PICKENHEIMER

APPETIZER

PERFECT POTATO PUSH

Appetizer Ingredients:

Master Chef:
- [ ] 2 wooden spoons
- [ ] 2 small potatoes
- [ ] Whistle

Student Chefs: (Four or more players)
- ✗ No materials required

Appetizer Preparation:

None required.

Appetizer Activity:

Divide the children into Team A and Team B. Then say:

> Team A, separate into two sides. Line up facing each other with about 15 feet of space between both lines. *(Pause for the children to follow this instruction.)* Team B will now do the same thing. *(Pause for the children to follow this instruction.)*

Give a wooden spoon and a potato to the first person in line for each team. Then say:

> When I blow the whistle, the person with the wooden spoon will push the potato with the spoon to his or her team member in the opposite line. Then that person will go to the back of the line. The next team member will do the same thing. We will continue the game until all the team members have pushed the potato with the spoon. The team who does this the fastest wins the game.

PRECISE AND POLITE POT PIE

Main Course Ingredients:

Master Chef:
- ☐ *Prudence Primrose Pickenheimer* story (pages 62-63)

Student Chefs:
- ✗ No materials required

Main Course Preparation:

None required.

Main Course Activity:

Read the following story aloud to the children. Pause at the involvement questions for the children's answers.

Prudence Primrose Pickenheimer

Prudence Primrose Pickenheimer
was perfect as perfect could be.
She lived in a perfect little house
shaded by a perfect little tree.

Her perfect little dresses
matched the perfect little bows
she placed in her perfect hair
in perfect little rows.

Her bright and perfect smile
showed her perfect pearly teeth.
And with eyes a perfect brown,
Prudence looked especially sweet.

Her words were kind and graceful;
perfectly spoken, delightfully clear.
As soft as a gentle whisper,
yet loud enough to hear.

Prudence Primrose Pickenheimer
seemed perfect in every way.
But her perfect world was shattered
one *not-so-perfect* day.

STOP Ask the children: "What do you think happened?"

It seemed each year that Prudence
had been the TOP student in each grade.
She had earned only raspberry stickers
for the perfect marks that she'd made.

Strawberry stickers were great to have,
and cherry ones better, I guess.
But for Perfect Prudence raspberry stickers
meant perfection at its best!

But today when the class got stickers,
something seemed perfectly odd.
The raspberry sticker didn't go to Prudence,
but to Theodore Thaddeus McClodd!

The second one went
to Millicent McHurst.
How could this happen?
Prudence always was first!

STOP Ask the children: "Which sticker did Prudence want? Why?"

After Wykeeta's raspberry sticker,
Prudence's name was called.
But Wykeeta and Prudence's stickers
were not the same at all.

"There must be some mistake,"
Prudence whispered in her perfect little voice.
"For this cherry sticker in my hand
is not the sticker of my choice."

Her teacher quietly assured her
that no mistake was made,
and that she'd earned that cherry sticker
for her cherry sticker grade.

Then Prudence Primrose Pickenheimer
felt a sudden and awful chill.
The cherry sticker in her hand
had made her perfectly ill.

STOP Ask the children: "What is Prudence's problem?"

Prudence hurried to her perfect home
quickly as could be.
She made her way onto her perfect porch
shaded by a perfect little tree.

Her mom sat down beside her and asked,
"Is something wrong, my dear?"
Her mother's words were softly spoken;
gentle, yet perfectly clear.

"Oh, Mom, it was just awful," said Prudence
in her perfect little voice.
"Today I received a CHERRY sticker,
and raspberry is my choice.

"Since kindergarten, I have always been
the top student in each grade.
I have earned only raspberry stickers
for the perfect marks I've made."

STOP Ask the children: "Why was Prudence upset?"

"Growing up is not always easy," Mom said,
"nor the changes getting older will bring.
But as you grow, remember, dear,
this one important thing …

"Being perfect, my sweet Prudence,
is not what you say or do.
You are perfect in every way
just because you are you!

"True happiness will come to you
when you've learned to accept your best,
whether it's a raspberry or cherry sticker
for the marks on ANY test!"

Prudence and Mom sat and talked
on the porch by the perfect little tree
until the moonlight kissed the dark blue sky
and the starlight they could see.

The next day, the world seemed brighter.
Birds sang from every tree.
And Prudence felt perfectly happy,
'cause Prudence felt perfectly free.

STOP Ask the children: "Are things better for Prudence now?"

Prudence still wears her perfect little dresses,
and matches them with perfect little bows.
But Prudence no longer places them
in perfect little rows!

SUGARLESS NO-STRESS STRING ART

Dessert Ingredients:

Master Chef:
- ☐ Stapler and staples
- ☐ Ribbon
- ☐ Chalkboard and chalk (optional)

Student Chefs:
- ☐ Copy of *Bows* (page 65) for each girl
- ☐ Copy of *Bow Ties* (page 66) for each boy
- ☐ Markers
- ☐ Scissors
- ☐ Glue
- ☐ Glitter

Dessert Preparation:

Make a copy of *Bows* for each girl. Make a copy of *Bow Ties* for each boy.

Dessert Activity:

Distribute scissors, markers, glue, glitter, and either *Bows* or *Bow Ties* to each child. Then say:

Take your marker and write one word from this sentence on each bow or bow tie: ***It's perfectly perfect not to be perfect.*** *(For younger children, you may wish to write the sentence on the board.)* Then cut out each bow or bow tie. When you have completed this task, raise your hand. I will call you to the front of the room so you can staple your bows or bow ties onto a piece of ribbon. You should begin your stapling with the word ***It's*** and end with the word ***perfect*** so that when you hang the ribbon up, you can read the sentence. After the bows or bow ties are stapled to the ribbon, sprinkle the ribbon with glue and glitter. Then set it aside to dry. When the ribbon is dry, you may hang your masterpiece in a special place.

BOWS

BOW TIES

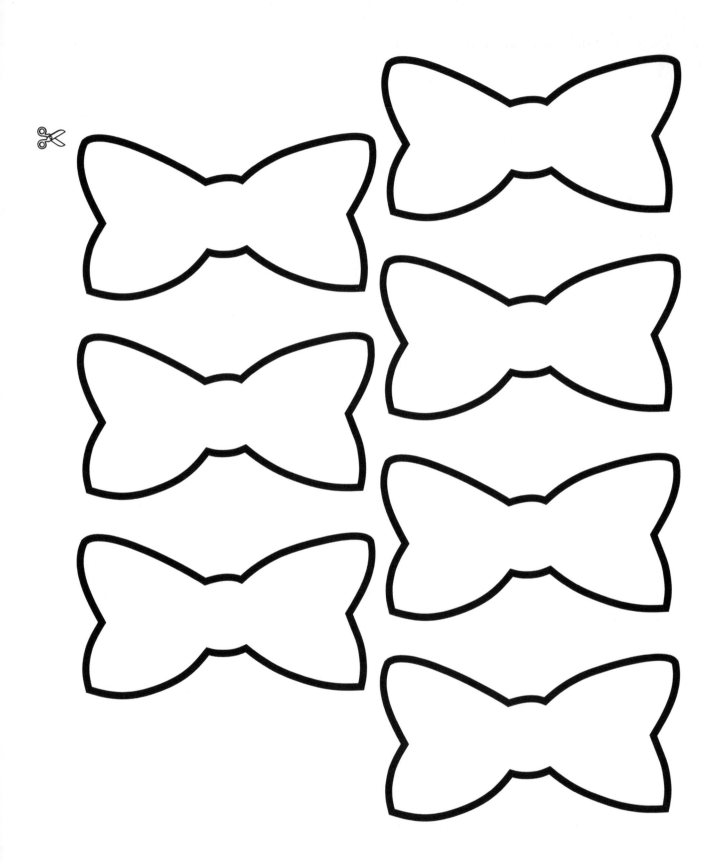

GUIDANCE FOR THE GOURMET © 2006 MAR★CO PRODUCTS, INC. 1-800-448-2197

JACK TALKS BACK

APPETIZER

ORNERY HAM SCRAMBLES

Appetizer Ingredients:

Master Chef:
- ☐ Copy of *Respectful Rules* (pages 72-82)
- ☐ Card stock
- ☐ Scissors
- ☐ Marker
- ☐ Envelopes equal to the number of rules being used
- ☐ Timer
- ☐ Chalkboard and chalk

Student Chefs: (12 or more players)
- ✗ No materials required

Appetizer Preparation:

Make a copy of *Respectful Rules* on cardstock or heavy-weight paper. Cut apart the strips. You may use the blank strips to write your own rule. (***Note:*** Each rule consists of six words.)

Suggested rules are:

- Stay in your seat and work.
- Ask permission to leave the room.
- Use a polite voice in class.
- Be respectful to adults and classmates.
- Never use put-downs or hurtful words.
- Listen to all your teacher's instructions.
- Do not poke, pinch, or push.
- Do not cause problems in class.
- Be respectful of other people's opinions.
- Don't interrupt when others are speaking.

Cut apart the words from each sentence strip. Place the words in an envelope.

Appetizer Activity:

Divide the children into groups of six. Then say:

These envelopes contain words that, if put together correctly, will make a sentence about being respectful. Each envelope contains six words, one for each member of your group. I will call each group to the front of the room and give each group member a word from the envelope. When I tell the group members to start, they will arrange themselves in a line, holding up the words, so the mixed-up words make up a respectful rule. I will time each group to see who can do this most quickly.

Begin the activity, recording on the chalkboard the time each group spends to correctly arrange the words into a rule.

(***Note:*** For smaller groups, cut the words apart, scramble them, and place them on the table or desk. Then allow the children to put them in order. Again, the children who complete the task most quickly win the game.)

OH-SO-SASSY SALMON SURPRISE

Main Course Ingredients:

Master Chef:
☐ *Jack Talks Back* story (pages 68-70)

Student Chefs:
✗ No materials required

Main Course Preparation:

None required.

Main Course Activity:

Read the following story aloud to the children. Pause at the involvement questions for the children's answers.

Jack Talks Back

Jack is a bright little fellow
who can do most anything.
He's a whiz at chess, bowls the best,
and like a bird this lad can sing.

He plays both harp and piano,
and does it with style and flair.
His grades in school are impressive.
Seems no one can compare.

For bowling, chess, and making good grades,
he does have quite a knack.
But Jack has one big problem.
Jack simply loves to talk back.

STOP Ask the children: "What is Jack's problem?"

He talks back to his teacher.
He talks back to his mom.
And, according to Jack,
what he does is not wrong.

This morning his mom pleaded,
"Jack, please clean your room,"
"I can't," he replied, kicking things to the side,
"Joe and Mikey will be here soon.

"We have friends to visit
and a movie to see,
and I won't be home
'til a quarter past three."

"Clean your room now,"
said his mom with a shout.
"Clean it right now,
or you will not go out!"

"Mom, please," he said smugly,
"you don't have to scream.
I've already explained
why my room I won't clean.

"And what's the use?"
he replied with a grin.
"It's just going to get
all messy again."

STOP Ask the children: "Is Jack being respectful?"

When Mom asked Jack
to rake the leaves,
"I can't," he griped.
"I might start to sneeze.

"Just suppose I agreed,"
he did complain,
"to rake the leaves
and it started to rain?

"Then I'd get wet
and ruin my voice.
Now that would not
be a very wise choice.

"And besides, the yard
will get messy again,"
Jack said with that look
and smug grin again.

When the telephone rang
about four p.m.,
it was Jack's teacher,
Ms. Tina McTim.

"The principal," she said,
"is on the other line.
Please ma'am, we need
just a bit of your time."

STOP Ask the children: "Why do you think the principal and Jack's teacher are calling?"

"You see," she began, "Jack has talent
and can do many things.
At golf and chess he is the best,
he bowls as well as he sings.

"He plays both harp and piano
and does it with style and flair.
His grades are most impressive.
Seems no one can compare.

"For golf, chess, and making good grades,
he does have quite a knack.
But Jack has one big problem,
Jack simply loves to talk back."

The principal chimed in,
"We must set things straight.
Behavior like this
we can not tolerate!

"So please," she implored,
"you must make the time
to meet with us here
at a quarter past nine."

Mom went to that meeting.
Dad was there, too.
Dad listened, then spoke,
"I know just what to do."

After the meeting,
Dad sat down with Jack.
"Son, Mom and your teacher
say you like to talk back."

"Not so," said Jack,
with the greatest of ease.
"Dad, my teacher and Mom
talked back to me!

"Then they got all mad,
but I let it go,
because moms and teachers
are just girls, you know."

STOP Ask the children: "What do you think Jack meant by that remark?"

Well, Dad made it clear
that mommies and teachers
would be respected
just like all of earth's creatures.

And that Jack's mom and teacher
were not merely girls,
but important people
who helped shaped his world.

Dad explained things to Jack
like only dads can.
And when Dad finished,
Jack was a changed young man.

STOP Ask the children: "What do you think Jack's dad said to Jack?"

Oh, he still plays chess,
he golfs and he sings,
plays harp and piano,
makes good grades and things.

But now when Mom speaks,
Jack doesn't talk back.

He no longer gives her
his yakkity-yak!

Since that nine fifteen meeting,
Jack's not been the same,
his teacher and Mom
both gladly exclaimed.

Dad helped him see that
what he once did was wrong.
Now this talented fellow
sings a brand new song.

FINISH the story by asking the children: "Did Jack change? How do you know?"

POLITE PIE STREAMERS

Dessert Ingredients:

Master Chef:
- ☐ Stapler and staples or glue

Student Chefs:
- ☐ Paper plates
- ☐ Crepe paper or tissue paper
- ☐ Markers
- ☐ Scissors

Dessert Preparation:

None required.

Dessert Activity:

Distribute scissors, a paper plate, crepe paper or tissue paper, and a marker to each child. Then say:

Cut the middle out of the paper plate. Using a marker, write polite things to say to adults around the edges of the paper plate. You might say, "Good morning, Thank you, Please, Excuse me, May I? or anything else that would be a polite saying." Then cut long, flowing streamers from your crepe paper/tissue paper. When you have finished, come to my desk and staple/glue the streamers onto the plate. Then you may give this colorful gift to an adult.

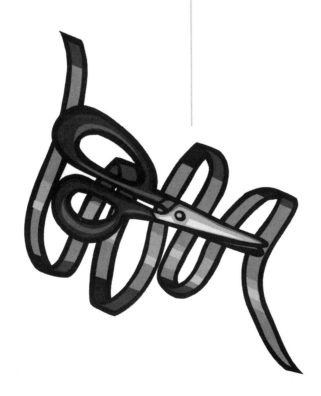

STAY

IN

YOUR

SEAT

AND

WORK

ASK

PERMISSION

TO

LEAVE

THE

ROOM

USE

A

POLITE

VOICE

IN

CLASS

BE

RESPECTFUL

TO

ADULTS

AND

CLASSMATES

NEVER

USE

PUT-DOWNS

OR

HURTFUL

WORDS

LISTEN

TO

ALL

YOUR

TEACHER'S

INSTRUCTIONS

DO

NOT

POKE

PINCH

OR

PUSH

DO

NOT

CAUSE

PROBLEMS

IN

CLASS

BE

RESPECTFUL

OF

OTHER

PEOPLE'S

OPINIONS

DON'T

INTERRUPT

WHEN

OTHERS

ARE

SPEAKING

NORMA-NELL, TATTLETALE

APPETIZER

TATTLE OR TELL CHEDDAR TALES

Appetizer Ingredients:

Master Chef:
- ☐ Copy of *Tattling Or Telling Strips* (pages 88-89)
- ☐ Marker
- ☐ Scissors
- ☐ 2 cupcake tins
- ☐ Small box
- ☐ Timer
- ☐ Chalkboard and chalk

Student Chefs: (2 or more players)
- ✗ No materials required

Appetizer Preparation:

Make a copy of the *Tattling Or Telling Strips* or write your own examples of *tattling* or *telling* on strips of paper. Cut apart the strips. Place the strips in the small box. On one cupcake tin, write: *Tell.* On the other, write: *Tattle.*

Appetizer Activity:

Introduce the activity by saying:

> I am going to give these strips of paper to one player at a time. When I say, "Go," he or she is to read the strip, decide if what is written on the strip describes *tattling* or *telling,* and place the strip in the correct tin. I will time each player, and the player who completes the task most quickly will be the winner.

Select the first player. Record the amount of time it took him/her to complete the task on the chalkboard. Collect the strips and put them in the box. Shake the box and continue with the next player. Continue until each child has had a chance to play.

(***Note:*** For younger children, read the words, then have the child place the strip in the correct cupcake tin.)

TATTLE-TATTLE TELL ALL TORTELLINI

Main Course Ingredients:

Master Chef:
- [ ] *Norma-Nell Tattletale story* (pages 84-86)

Student Chefs:
- ✗ No materials required

Main Course Preparation:

None required.

Main Course Activity:

Read the following story aloud to the children. Pause at the involvement questions for the children's answers.

Norma-Nell Tattletale

"Ms. Nobel," yelled Norma-Nell,
"guess what I saw Tyler do?
He hid bubble gum under his tongue
after you told him not to chew!

"He broke Trina's pencil
and wrote in Sam's book.
And at Tommy's test,
he took a quick look!

Ms. Nobel!

"And then during lunch,
he ate Freida's fries
and stared at my ice cream
and Mitchell's apple pie!

"When we had recess,
he piled rocks on the slide.
Then I am told,
he threw dirt in Joe's eye.

"Well, he didn't really throw it,
but Tom thought that he might.
'Cause he did it to Marge.
Trish told him last night.

"He broke Kate's crayons,
and Meisha Brown's, too.
That's when I decided
I was gonna tell you."

"Thanks," said Ms. Nobel.
"I can count on you, Norma,
to always be
my hourly informer."

STOP Ask the children: "What is Norma's problem?"

"Remember that we talked
about when we should tell?"
Ms. Nobel whispered to Norma
at the sound of the bell.

"We tell when there's danger
or if someone is hurt.
But not when a friend
stares at your dessert!"

STOP Ask the children: "How is *tattling* different from *telling*?"

"Please remember this, Norma.
Don't forget what I say.

It may come in handy.
It may help you one day."

But Norma-Nell
did not change her ways.
She continued tattling
the very next day.

"Ms. Nobel, I heard that
Ike, Trish, and Lynn
told Sara they were
no longer my friends.

"Then they told Naomi
they hated my dress,
that my new shoes were silly,
and so was my vest."

"You tattle too much,"
cried Jen and JP.
"Norma, please stop!"
begged Margaret-Marie.

But that didn't stop Norma.
Her tattling got worse.
She blabbed to Ms. Nobel
and Ms. Friendly, the nurse.

It drove them all mad.
Something had to be done.
"Please stop her, someone!"
Begged Kaitlin and John.

"I have an idea,
Ms. Nobel," said Kristen.
"When Norma starts to tattle,
we just won't listen."

All quickly agreed
when she walked through the door.
Each time that she tattled,
she'd just be ignored.

Next day, she walked in
at eight o'clock on the dot.
"John's finger," she whined
"is too close to my spot!

"He's looking at me
and touching my chair.
He breathed on my paper
and coughed in my hair!"

STOP Ask the children: "Do you think tattling is silly? Why?"

But all had agreed
when she walked through the door,
that each time that she tattled,
she'd just be ignored.

"Someone," she shouted,
"has used my eraser!"
Then she claimed that last night,
Dave's dog almost chased her.

But all had agreed
when she walked through the door,
that each time that she tattled,
she'd just be ignored.

Since no one would listen,
not even the nurse,
Norma packed up her books
and grabbed her red purse.

She sat on the bench
near the slide and oak tree.
Then she cried with a shout,
"No one listens to me!"

STOP Ask the children: "How is Norma-Nell feeling?"

Then said Ms. Nobel,
"I warned you, I fear,
that too much tattling
could hurt you, my dear."

"Will you help me, Ms. Nobel?
Will you help me today
to tell and not tattle
in class or at play?"

Ms. Nobel said,
"I do have a plan
I used it last year
with a student named Dan.

"When I see that you're tattling,
my left eye I will wink.
That should give you some time
to just stop and think!

"But if my right eye I wink,
and scratch my left ear,
just continue to speak,
what you say I will hear."

They practiced for weeks.
It was awkward at first.
But the tattling stopped,
their little plan worked!

Ms. Nobel was thrilled.
Ms. Friendly was, too.
And Norma-Nell felt proud
of what she'd learned NOT to do.

She now uses her talents
in a brand new way
by making morning announcements
for Ms. Nobel each day.

FINISH the story by asking the children: "What is Norma-Nell's new job?"

NO TATTLING BOOKMARK BEAUTIES

Dessert Ingredients:

Master Chef:
- ☐ Copy of *Bookmarks* (page 90)
- ☐ Cardstock
- ☐ Scissors
- ☐ Yarn
- ☐ Hole punch

Student Chefs:
- ☐ Glue
- ☐ Glitter
- ☐ Crayons or markers

Dessert Preparation:

Using cardstock, reproduce and cut out one bookmark for each child. Punch a hole in each bookmark.

Dessert Activity:

Introduce the activity by saying:

> Today, we are going to make bookmarks. They will remind you of your place in your book, and they will also remind you about *tattling* and *telling*.

Distribute a bookmark, glue, crayons or markers, and glitter to each child.

This is your bookmark. You may decorate and color it any way you wish. When you have finished, bring your bookmark to me and we will tie a piece of yarn to it.

BOOKMARKS

TELL WHAT'S IMPORTANT

TELL WHAT'S IMPORTANT

TELL WHAT'S IMPORTANT

90   GUIDANCE FOR THE GOURMET © 2006 MAR•CO PRODUCTS, INC. 1-800-448-2197

TATTLING OR TELLING STRIPS

Mary's cheating. I saw her look on Linda's paper.

Ken called me a "cry baby."

Tina and Shandi won't let me play.

Patty said she'd play with me and now she won't.

Jennie said she didn't like me any more.

Sela is making fun of my new outfit.

Gina and Laurie say they don't like me anymore.

Hans and Lenny run away when I come near them.

My lunch money is missing from my desk.

Brenda wants to fight with me after school.

TATTLING OR TELLING STRIPS

Josh picked up a cat and threw it over a fence.

Nick has a knife in his backpack.

Trish keeps calling my mom a bad name.

Lila poured ketchup all over my sandwich.

When we were playing Dodge Ball,
nobody would throw the ball to me.

Jack won't let me pick what I want to do
on our project.

Clark put crayon marks all over my paper
and ruined it.

Todd told everyone they would lose the game
if I was on their team.

Carlos deliberately tripped me in the cafeteria.
It's the third time this week.

Angie punched me in the arm so hard that
I dropped my books in a puddle.

BOOKMARKS

 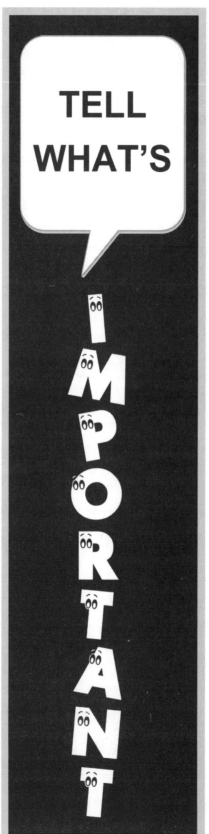 

IF YOU'RE HOME ALONE

APPETIZER

FAITHFUL FRUIT FLOATIES

Appetizer Ingredients:

Master Chef:
- ☐ Copy of *If You're Home Alone Situation/Action Strips* (pages 96-97)
- ☐ Scissors
- ☐ Balloons
- ☐ Balloon pump
- ☐ String

Student Chefs: (4 or more players—the larger the group, the better!)
- ✗ No materials required

Appetizer Preparation:

Make a copy of the *If You're Home Alone Situation/Action Strips.* Cut apart the strips, making sure that there is one strip for each participating student. Fold each strip and insert it into the mouth of a balloon. Use the balloon pump to blow each balloon up, then tie it off.

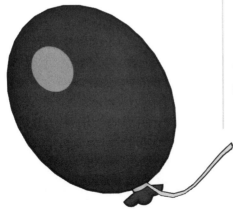

Appetizer Activity:

Show the children the balloons. Then introduce the activity by saying:

Inside each of these balloons is a strip of paper with something written on it. The paper either tells of something that could happen when you are home alone or the action you should take if you are home alone and the situation happens. Your task is to work together and match each situation with its appropriate action. I will give each of you a balloon. When I say, "Start," throw the balloons in the air and try to keep them afloat. When the first balloon falls to the floor, the task of keeping the balloons afloat is over. One child should burst the balloon on the floor and take the message out. The rest of you should each grab one balloon, burst it, and take the message out. Read your message, then find either the situation or the action that matches it. If you need help, you may use the number on the paper to find the strip with the same number. When everyone has matched his or her situation or action, you will share them with the group.

Give the children the signal to start. Play the game.

SAFE AND SECURE SAVORY STEW

Main Course Ingredients:

Master Chef:
☐ *If You're Home Alone* story (pages 92-94)

Student Chefs:
✗ No materials required

Main Course Preparation:

None required.

Main Course Activity:

Read the following story aloud to the children. Pause at the involvement questions for the children's answers.

If You're Home Alone

If the telephone rings
and your parents aren't home,
never let on
that you're there all alone.

Just take a message
and have a parent call back.
It's best to be safe,
and that is a fact.

STOP Ask the children: "What is your parents' rule about answering the phone when they are not home?"

If you get hungry
and there's no one around,
look in the fridge
to see what can be found.

Try munching on
crackers, fruit, celery, or cheese
until a parent returns:
No cooking, please.

If you're all alone
and someone knocks to come in,
don't say a word.
Don't answer, my friend.

Keep the door locked.
And if they won't go,
call a neighbor or another
grown-up you know.

If you're all alone
and you hear creepy sounds,
don't get upset.
Just settle down.

Ask yourself,
"Now what can this be?"
Be brave and say,
"I won't let it scare me!"

But if there is trouble,
leave there, don't stay.
Call for help
AFTER you get away.

STOP Ask the children: "If you had to leave your home, where would you go?"

If you're home alone
and start to feel bad,
pick up the phone
and call Mom or Dad.

Tell them what hurts.
Ask what to do.
Then do right away
what they tell you to.

Don't take any medicine.
Ask Mom or Dad first.
It could make you more sick.
It could make things worse.

If you're home alone
and you cut your finger,
don't be afraid.
The pain will not linger.

Wash the cut off
and bandage it well.
Your mom and dad
be sure to tell.

But if the cut is deep
and the bleeding won't stop,
press on it hard,
right on the top.

Use a clean cloth
or a clean tissue.
The bleeding should stop.
It shouldn't be an issue.

But if it won't stop,
you must call someone:
a neighbor, a friend,
or 9-1-1.

If you're home alone
and you don't understand
your math or your spelling,
just call a friend.

Ask for some help,
listen, and then try.
It's OK to get help.
No need to be shy.

STOP Ask the children: "Which friend would you call?"

If you're home alone
and it starts to storm,
stay safe inside.
No need for alarm.

Play with a puzzle
or your favorite game.
Soon you'll forget
the thunder and rain.

Being home alone is
a good place to learn
to care for yourself
until your parents return.

If you're all alone
and the lights all go out,
you'll need a flashlight.
So go fish it out.

First, talk with your parents
before they both go.
Ask where they are going,
so you will know.

If you are afraid,
pretend you're in space
or on a mission
in a secret, dark place.

If the lights aren't on soon,
don't even think twice
about using the phone
to ask your parent's advice.

STOP Ask the children: "What would your pretend mission be?"

If you're home alone
and make a big mess,
just learn what to do.
There is no need to stress.

Try to remember
what it looked like before
you threw all your stuff
all over the floor.

Put everything back
in its own special place.
Then try not to make
such a mess of the space.

But if you need help,
get on the phone.
Call a relative or neighbor
if they are at home.

Tell them what happened.
Ask what to do.
I'm sure they will
both gladly help you.

If you're all alone
and can't find what you need,
like your coat, your brush,
or a book you must read.

Think really hard about
where it could be.
Then look in those places.
That is the key!

When you do find it,
think, "Where should this go?"
Being organized
is helpful, you know.

STOP Ask the children: "Have you ever lost anything important?"

When you're all alone,
it's important for you
to follow the rules
like you're expected to do.

Your parents must know
that when they're not there,
you can be trusted
in your own care.

Don't disappoint them.
Make them feel proud.
Do what is right,
just like you vowed!

FINISH the story by asking the children: "How do you feel about being home alone?"

EMERGENCY PLAN PUDDING

Dessert Ingredients:

Master Chef:
- ☐ Stapler and staples

Student Chefs:
- ☐ Copy of *My Emergency Plan* booklet (pages 98-101)
- ☐ Pencil

Dessert Preparation:

Make a copy of *My Emergency Plan* for each child.

Dessert Activity:

Introduce the activity by saying:

> Each of you is going to make an *Emergency Plan* booklet. When you have finished, you may take it home and share it with your parents.

Give each child a booklet and a pencil. Guide the children, page by page, to complete the booklet. Staple the completed pages together and have the children take their booklets home.

(**Note:** If a child does not know the answers required for the pages, have him/her take the booklet home and have his/her parent(s) help complete it.)

1. **If you get sick**

2. **If you break a glass**

3. **If you are hungry**

4. **If there is a knock on the door**

5. **If you get scared**

6. **If you need help with your homework**

7. **If you get bored**

8. **If you scrape your knee**

9. **If you get upset**

10. **If you lose something**

11. **If there is an emergency**

12. **If the lights go out**

13. **If you hear a strange sound**

14. **If you can't reach your parents**

15. **If you want to break a rule**

1.	**call your parents**
2.	**clean it up**
3.	**eat a snack**
4.	**don't answer**
5.	**try to be brave**
6.	**call a friend**
7.	**do something fun**
8.	**wash it off**
9.	**try to calm down**
10.	**look for it**
11.	**call 9-1-1**
12.	**use a flashlight**
13.	**think what it might be**
14.	**call an adult whom you trust**
15.	**think about what will happen**

MY EMERGENCY PLAN

by

_____

GUIDANCE FOR THE GOURMET © 2006 MAR∗CO PRODUCTS, INC. 1-800-448-2197

All About Me

My Address _____

_____

_____

My Phone # (_____) _____

My Birth Date _____

Mom's & Dad's Phone Numbers

Mom's Cell # (_____) _____

Dad's Cell # (_____) _____

Mom's Work # (_____) _____

Dad's Work # (_____) _____

Other Phone Numbers For My Parents:

(_____) _____

(_____) _____

(_____) _____

(_____) _____

My Special Helpers

NAMES   **NUMBERS**

Relatives:

_____   (_____) _____

_____   (_____) _____

_____   (_____) _____

Neighbors:

_____   (_____) _____

_____   (_____) _____

_____   (_____) _____

Close Friends:

_____   (_____) _____

_____   (_____) _____

_____   (_____) _____

Emergency Helpers

Police Department   (_____) _____

Fire Department   (_____) _____

My Doctor   (_____) _____

My Emergency Checklist

First Aid Kit   ☐ YES   ☐ NO

Flashlight   ☐ YES   ☐ NO

Extra Batteries   ☐ YES   ☐ NO

Spare Key   ☐ YES   ☐ NO

_____   ☐ YES   ☐ NO

_____   ☐ YES   ☐ NO

_____   ☐ YES   ☐ NO

Other Special Stuff

_____

_____

_____

_____

Questions I Have

? _____ ?

_____

THE PINK SPOOKY MEN

APPETIZER

SPOOKY MAN SOUFFLE TOSS

Appetizer Ingredients:

Master Chef:
- ☐ Timer
- ☐ 2 pails
- ☐ 2 bean bags
- ☐ Chalkboard and chalk

Student Chefs: (4 or more players)
- ✘ No materials required

Appetizer Preparation:

Draw a chalk line to be the starting line. Place the pails at a distance at which it will be challenging, but not impossible, for children this age to score.

Appetizer Activity:

Introduce the activity by saying:

I will divide you into two teams. Two players from each team will try to earn points at the same time. One player will stand near the starting line to toss the bean bag into the pail. The other player will stand behind the pail in order to quickly retrieve the bean bag and get it back to the tosser. Each time the bean bag lands in the pail, the team is awarded two points. The retriever must quickly return the bean bag to the tosser, so the team can earn more points. These players will have one minute to make as many points as they can for their team. After one minute has elapsed, two new members of each team will have a chance to toss and retrieve the bean bag. The game will end after each player has had a chance to toss or retrieve the bean bag. The points will be tallied, and the team with the most points will be the winner.

Divide the children into two teams and begin the game. Record points on the chalkboard as they are earned.

FEARLESS FLOUNDER FILLETS

Main Course Ingredients:

Master Chef:
- ☐ *The Pink Spooky Men* story (pages 103-106)

Student Chefs:
- ✗ No materials required

Main Course Preparation:

None required.

Main Course Activity:

Read the following story aloud to the children. Pause at the involvement questions for the children's answers.

The Pink Spooky Men

In an imaginary place called Spookyman Land, there are all kinds of Spookymen …

Some have warts.
Some have wings.
And some have
awful, squiggly things.

But the strangest one in all the land was the Pink Spookyman.

Because the Pink Spookyman was different, the Spookymen with warts, wings, and squiggly things were very unkind to him.

Each morning, they zoomed around him as he walked to school, teasing him and saying …

"Phoney baloney,
rink-dink-dink.
Real Spookymen
are not pink!

"Skedaddle, skadiddle
as fast as you can.
You're not wanted
in Spookyman Land."

Being teased made the Pink Spookyman a little grumpy. But at school, Mrs. Snoutnewt, their new teacher, saw to it that the Spookymen all settled down and behaved themselves like proper Spookymen should.

In Spookyman class, they learned to moan like Spookymen moan. They learned to howl like Spookymen howl. They learned to snarl like Spookymen snarl. And they learned to gnash their teeth like Spookymen gnash teeth.

The Pink Spookyman tried very hard to be a proper Spookyman. But when he tried to moan, he mooed like a cow! And when he tried to howl, he barked like a dog! He tried to snarl, and nearly choked! He tried gnashing his teeth, and bit his tongue!

The Pink Spookyman felt terribly silly; but feeling silly was nothing new for the Pink Spookyman.

STOP Ask the children: "Why was the Pink Spookyman feeling so silly?"

When the school day ended, all the Spookymen met at Slime Lake to munch on earthworm sandwiches and slurp caterpillar soup. Then they played tag in the lake's thick, green water until it was time to go.

The Pink Spookyman watched from the willow tree that hung over the green lake. How he wished he could play with the others! But an old wooden sign near the squeaky park bench read …

KEEP OUT IF YOU ARE PINK!

Soon the sky turned dark and gloomy. That meant homework time in Spookyman Land. So the Spookymen with warts, wings, and squiggly things read the Naughty List Mrs. Snoutnewt had given them. Then they made their way through the thick fog and into the next town to creep through the windows of sleeping children and do what proper Spookymen do best.

The Pink Spookyman read his list, then quietly slipped away.

STOP Ask the children: "How do you think the Pink Spookyman is feeling now?"

Aaron Applegate was first on the Spookymen's list this night. At his sister's party, he had stuck a big, green lizard on her pretty birthday cake and a fat, lumpy toad in her ice cream sundae.

Sarah Sloan was also on that list. While her grandma and grandpa were napping, she shaved their fluffy white cat and glued the fur to their noisy canary.

So the Spookymen crept through Aaron and Sarah's windows. They moaned. They howled. They snarled and they gnashed their big teeth!

When Aaron and Sarah promised never to be naughty again, the Spookymen went away.

The last name on the list was Haskel H. Hinkley, but it seemed Haskel H. Hinkley had done nothing wrong. Still, the Spookymen crept through his window and moaned, howled, snarled, and gnashed their big teeth.

When Haskel H. Hinkley heard the noisy Spookymen he sat up, Then he stood tall, very tall, in his little bed.

He moaned like the Spookymen moaned … only longer.

And howled like the Spookymen howled … only louder.

And snarled like the Spookymen snarled … only deeper.

And gnashed his big teeth like the Spookymen gnashed theirs … only better!

Then he slapped each of their big, scaly hands.

"What did you go and do that for?" the Spookymen sniffled, wiping away big Spookyman tears.

"That's for drooling on my bed!" yelled Haskel H. Hinkley.

STOP Ask the children: "Why do you think Haskel H. Hinkley was not afraid of the mean Spookymen?"

The next morning, the Spookymen with warts, wings, and squiggly things talked with Mrs. Snoutnewt about Haskel H. Hinkley. She listened, then smiled like only Mrs. Snoutnewt could. You see, she had three extra lips and an extra set of teeth. Then she said, "Perhaps you should try to be better Spookymen."

The Spookymen looked confused. They looked at Mrs. Snoutnewt. Then they looked at each other. "But we're already the best," they said quietly but proudly.

Things were even more confusing later at Slime Lake. That's when the Spookymen with warts, wings, and squiggly things learned that the only name on their list for the night was Haskel H. Hinkley.

The Spookymen were shaken, still they had to be brave. So they crept through the fog and back to his room.

And this time, they moaned longer.

And they howled louder.

They snarled deeper.

And they gnashed their big teeth even better than they had before.

Haskel H. Hinkley laughed out loud when he saw the clumsy Spookymen. Then he stretched his arms toward the sky and began to grow. He grew and he grew and he grew! Then he roared the roar of fifty lions and nearly blew the Spookymen away. The frightened Spookymen's knees started knocking. They yelled real loudly for their mothers.

STOP Ask the children: "Why did the Spookymen yell for their mothers?"

As the Spookymen with warts, wings, and squiggly things walked to school the next morning, a very large and a very loud Haskel H. Hinkley whizzed around them, shouting …

"Phoney baloney,
rink-dink-dink.
You Spookymen are not
as brave as you think!
Skedaddle, skadiddle
as fast as you can
or I'll chase *you* away
from Spookyman Land!

The Spookymen wanted to stand up to Haskel H. Hinkley. But when they tried to moan, they mooed like cows. And when they tried to howl, they barked like dogs. They tried snarling, and nearly choked. They tried gnashing their teeth, and they bit their tongues!

The Spookymen felt terribly silly; but for the Spookymen with warts, wings, and squiggly things feeling silly was nothing new anymore.

At Slime Lake later that afternoon, none of the Spookymen ate earthworm sandwiches and none of them slurped caterpillar soup. Instead, they sat on the squeaky park bench near the thick, green lake and talked about Haskel H. Hinkley.

"I don't like it," said the Spookyman with warts, "when he says we're not brave."

"And I don't like it," said the Spookyman with wings, "when he says he'll chase us away."

"And I don't like it," said the Spookyman with squiggly things, "when he yells at us. It makes it hard to be a proper Spookyman."

At that moment, the Pink Spookyman slid slowly from the willow tree and stood in the middle of the group.

"I think I have a plan," the Pink Spookyman said bravely.

The Spookymen with warts, wings, and squiggly things looked at the Pink Spookyman and felt ashamed. For they finally understood what Mrs. Snoutnewt meant by being BETTER Spookymen.

STOP Ask the children: "What do you think Mrs. Snoutnewt meant?"

With the moon now high in the sky, the Pink Spookyman led the Spookymen with warts, wings, and squiggly things back to the room of Haskel H. Hinkley.

The Pink Spookyman stood near Haskel H. Hinkley's bed, and the Spookymen with warts, wings, and squiggly things stayed very close to each other and very close to the open window. Then, all together, they moaned, howled, snarled, and gnashed their teeth until the whole house rumbled.

Haskel H. Hinkley heard the fuss and slowly opened his red, sleepy eyes. He stared long and hard at the Pink Spookyman. Then, suddenly, Haskel H. Hinkley's red eyes became as big as the moon that lit the sky and as bright as the stars around it. He sat up, stood tall—very tall in his little bed—and leapt toward the Pink Spookyman.

The Spookymen with warts, wings, and squiggly things couldn't bear to look! Haskel H. Hinkley flung his long, strong arms around the thick neck of the Pink Spookyman and gave him a great big enormous … HUG. "Uncle Pinkanelleus," said Haskel H. Hinkley happily. "I thought you'd never come!"

At that moment, Mrs. Snoutnewt appeared with another Spookyman. One who roared the roar of fifty lions and was very tall, very strong, and very pink! Haskel H. Hinkley looked at Mrs. Snoutnewt, then he looked at the other Pink Spookyman. "Mom, Dad," he said excitedly, "Uncle Pinkanelleus is here!"

STOP Ask the children: "What is happening?"

Two Pink Spookymen? Mrs. Snoutnewt? Uncle Pinkanelleus? All the excitement was a little bit too much for the Spookymen with warts, wings, and squiggly things. As they stood near Haskel H. Hinkley's window with their mouths open and their tongues wagging, they fainted!

Since that night, things in Spookyman Land have never been the same.

MARSHMALLOW MASK MARMALADE

Dessert Ingredients:

Master Chef:
- ☐ Newspaper
- ☐ Various colors of paint
- ☐ Paint brushes
- ☐ Paint pans
- ☐ Decorative items such as markers, beads, glitter, buttons, yarn, and ribbons
- ☐ Gluesticks
- ☐ Elastic bands or craft sticks
- ☐ Stapler and staples

Student Chefs:
- ☐ Paper plate
- ☐ Pencil
- ☐ Scissors

Dessert Preparation:

Cover two tables with newspaper. Set out a selection of paints in paint pans and brushes on one table. On the other table, set out the decorative items and gluesticks.

Dessert Activity:

Give each child a paper plate, a pencil, and scissors. Then say:

Today, we are going to make masks. With a pencil, draw eyes on your paper plate. Then use your scissors and cut eye holes for your mask. When you have finished, come to the paint table and paint your mask. Then set it aside to dry. When your mask is dry, come to the craft table and, using glue, decorate your mask with whatever items you wish. On the inside of your mask, write the words: "No Fear."

When your mask is finished, I will staple an elastic band to it so you can wear it.

Have the children put on a parade to show off their masks to other classes.

(**Note:** Instead of using elastic bands, the paper plates may be glued or stapled to craft sticks.)

EAT YOUR BROCCOLI, IRENE

APPETIZER

FINICKY MINI-MORSELS

Appetizer Ingredients:

Master Chef:
- ☐ Copy of *Food Strips* (pages 114-117)
- ☐ Butcher paper
- ☐ Scissors
- ☐ Crayons
- ☐ Basket
- ☐ Tape
- ☐ Table

Student Chefs: (4 or more players)
- ✗ None required

Appetizer Preparation:

Make a copy of the *Food Strips.* Cut apart the strips. Put the strips of paper into the basket. From the butcher paper, cut a giant circle to use as a plate. Place the basket filled with *Food Strips*, a large piece of butcher paper, scissors, and crayons on a table. Tape the large circle to the floor in the front of the room.

Appetizer Activity:

Introduce the activity by saying:

This basket contains strips of paper with the names and pictures of different foods. Each of you will draw a strip of paper from the basket, then go to the butcher paper and draw a giant picture of the food that is on your strip of paper. Then you will cut out your picture and we will tape it to your chest. You will become "food folk."

When everyone has become "food folk," I will call one of you up to stand on the giant plate. That person will call up other "food folk" that would make his or her ideal, delicious meal. Then I will call another student to the front of the room and repeat the process. We will continue the game until everyone has had an opportunity to part of an ideal meal. (***Note:*** This activity is strictly for fun. Students will learn about food choices later in the lesson.)

Begin the game.

JIFFY NO-JUNK JAMBALAYA

Main Course Ingredients:

Master Chef:
☐ *Eat Your Broccoli, Irene* story
(pages 109-112)

Student Chefs:
☐ Drawing paper
☐ Crayons or markers

Main Course Preparation:

None required.

Main Course Activity:

Distribute drawing paper and crayons or markers to the children. Then read the following story aloud. Pause at the involvement questions for the children's answers.

Eat Your Broccoli, Irene

Dinner time was not a happy time for Irene or her family. Try as they might, Irene's family could not get her to eat the foods she should.

"Eat your broccoli," begged Mom.

"Eat your fruit," begged Dad.

"Eat your potatoes," begged her brother.

"Eat your tomatoes," begged Gran.

But Irene's answer was always the same:

"I like fries, I like chips,
and I like anything that's sweet.
For breakfast, lunch, and dinner,
that's all I'll ever eat.

"Not broccoli or potatoes.
Nothing healthy will I eat.
Not fresh fruit or tomatoes.
Just fries, chips, and anything sweet."

STOP Ask the children: "What seems to be the problem?"

"Have it your way, Irene," warned her mother. "But one day, all of that junk food is going to grow on you."

But Irene would not listen.

STOP Ask the children: "Did Irene take her mother's warning seriously?"

Irene watched TV instead. While she watched, she munched on ten chocolate chip cookies, nine lollipops, eight jawbreakers, seven candy bars, six donuts, five cupcakes, four bags of chips, three cream puffs, two bags of fries, and one hot dog. Then she fell asleep.

When Irene awoke the next morning, she wiped the chocolate from her mouth and brushed the crumbs from her bed. She put her leftover treats back into her goody drawer and stumbled to the bathroom to wash her face. When she looked in the mirror, she couldn't believe what she saw.

There were cookies growing from her ears, fries growing in her hair, donuts growing from her arms, cupcakes growing on her tummy, cream puffs growing on her thighs, and a hot dog growing from her nose!

STOP Say: Wow! Draw a picture of how Irene looked.

She tried plucking them off, but that didn't work.

She tried washing them off, but that didn't work.

She tried eating them off, but even that didn't work.

So Irene screamed! Then she looked in the mirror and screamed again.

Up Mom ran.
Up Dad ran.
Up ran her brother,
and up hobbled Gran!

They saw Irene. They screamed, too, right before they fainted. Everyone that is except Mom.

STOP Ask the children: "Why was Mom not surprised?"

"I told you, Irene," Mom scolded, "that one day all of that junk food would grow on you. It finally did. There is nothing we can do now. Get dressed and we will figure out what to do after school." Then Mom helped the others up from the floor.

"School?" asked Dad.

"School?" asked her brother.

"School?" asked Gran.

"SCHOOL?" screamed Irene.

"SCHOOL!" answered Mom.

Mom tried to help Irene get dressed. But because of all the junk food Irene had eaten, her dresses would not fit. They were too small.

So they tried Mom's dresses. But Mom's dresses were too small for Irene. They tried Gran's dresses, but Gran's dresses were too small, too. They even tried a neighbor's dresses, but they were too small. So Mom called Aunt Bertha. Aunt Bertha's dresses fit just right.

STOP Ask the children: "Why do you think Aunt Bertha's dresses fit Irene?"

When Irene got to school, the children stared at her, but pretended not to see the cookies in her ears, the fries in her hair, the donuts on her arms, the cupcakes on her tummy, the cream puffs on her thighs, and that hot dog on her nose.

All the children, that is, except for Jeremy!

"Mustard with that hot dog, Irene?" he smirked, causing the other children to howl with laughter.

"You silly boy," thought Irene, trying to ignore him and her snickering classmates.

Then she shuffled to her desk and squeezed herself into her seat. But she got stuck, and Mr. Washington, the custodian, had to help get her out.

STOP Ask the children: "Why did Mr. Washington have to help her?"

After that, her day got even worse. Some mean kids on the playground began to point at her, tease her, and call her ugly names because…

She was too big for the swings, too heavy for the teetertotter, too wide for the slide, and too tired to play tag.

To make things even worse, a hungry dog chased her all the way home, trying to eat the hot dog on her nose.

STOP Tell the children: "Irene is not having a good day. What do you think will happen next?"

"How did I get myself into this mess?" sighed Irene.

To make herself feel better, she wobbled up to her room and went straight to her goody drawer. She was about to gobble a handful of jellybeans when Mom called.

"Irene," she said, "we have a visitor. It's Doctor Eatwell. Come down and let him have a look at you."

Irene clunked down the stairs and shook hands with the doctor. Then the examination began.

"Hmmm," said Doctor Eatwell. He peered intently over his glasses while jiggling the donuts that hung from Irene's arms. "This looks serious, very serious indeed."

"What seems to be the problem, Doctor?" asked Irene's mother.

"Well," the good doctor answered …

"She ate fries, chips,
and anything sweet.
When you were not looking,
that's all she'd ever eat.

"Not broccoli or potatoes.
Nothing healthy would she eat.
Not fresh fruit or tomatoes.
Just fries, chips, and anything sweet."

STOP Ask the children: "Do you think Doctor Eatwell can help Irene?"

"What can we do?" asked Mother.

"Well," said Doctor Eatwell, fumbling in his bag, "I do believe I have a cure, but it may seem like bad medicine to you, Irene."

Doctor Eatwell took out his pad and wrote a prescription for Irene and her mother. "Follow all of my instructions and I will see you in two weeks," he said. Then he picked up his bag and his umbrella and closed the door behind him.

Mom read the prescription.

Monday: broccoli and fruit

Tuesday: skip around the block

Wednesday: potatoes and tomatoes with water 'round the clock

Thursday: fresh fruit and veggies

Friday: jog down the street

Saturday: lettuce, tomatoes, and a lean piece of meat

Sunday: stretch, relax, and get ready to repeat.

"The doctor was right," thought Irene. "It is bad medicine!"

"You can do it," said Mother.

"You can do it," said Father.

"You can do it," said her brother.

"You can do it," said Gran.

"I can do it," said Irene.

STOP Ask the children: "Do you think Irene will follow the doctor's instructions?"

So she ate the broccoli and the fruit and she skipped around the block, ate potatoes and tomatoes with water 'round the clock. She ate fresh fruit and veggies and jogged right down the street. She ate lettuce, tomatoes, and a lean piece of meat. Then she stretched, relaxed, and got ready to repeat.

When Doctor Eatwell returned …

Cookies were no longer growing from Irene's ears, fries were no longer growing in her hair, donuts were no longer growing from her arms, cupcakes were no longer growing on her tummy, cream puffs were no longer growing on her thighs, and that hot dog no longer grew from her nose!

STOP Ask the children: "Did the prescription work?"

Irene loved the way she looked. And she worked hard to stay that way.

So did Mom.
So did Dad.
So did her brother.
And so did Gran.

But every now and then, after she has eaten her broccoli, fruit, potatoes, and tomatoes and after she has skipped around the block and jogged down the street, Irene still enjoyed a few chips and a tiny sweet treat.

So did Dad.
So did her brother.
So did Gran.
And so did Mother.

FINISH the story by asking the children: "Do you think is it OK to have chips and sweets every now and then? Why?"

WHOLESOME HONEY TREATS

Dessert Ingredients:

Master Chef:
- ☐ Table
- ☐ Decorative items such as markers, beads, glitter, buttons, yarn, and ribbons
- ☐ Gluesticks
- ☐ Newspaper
- ☐ Magnetic tape
- ☐ Chalkboard and chalk

Student Chefs:
- ☐ 4 index cards
- ☐ Pencil

Dessert Preparation:

Cover the table with newspaper and set out the gluesticks and decorative items. Write the following on the chalkboard:

Breakfast: fruit, yogurt, oatmeal, muffins, eggs, cereal, cheese, toast, milk

Lunch: broccoli, pizza, pasta, chicken, bread, apple, sandwich, baked chips

Dinner: green beans, corn, fish, yams, banana, cottage cheese, tomatoes

Snack: apple, pecans, carrots, raisins, crackers, grapes, celery, peanut butter

Make a sample *Personalized Menu Card* to show the students.

Sample Personalized Menu Card

Connie's Choice
(My Breakfast Menu)

milk, cereal, fruit,
breakfast bar, boiled egg,
bagel, oatmeal

Dessert Activity:

Give each child four index cards and a pencil. Then say:

Today, you are going to make four *Personalized Menu Cards*. One for breakfast, one for lunch, one for dinner, and one for a snack. Choose your menus from the list on the board. If a wholesome food that you like is not mentioned on the list, you may use it on your menu. When you have completed your menus, bring them to the table to decorate them.

When you have finished, bring your menu to me. I will stick a piece of magnetic tape to each menu and you may take your menu home and stick it to your refrigerator as a reminder of the right foods to eat.

VEGETABLE

VEGETABLE

VEGETABLE

FRUIT

FRUIT

FRUIT

PASTA

PASTA

MEAT

MEAT

FISH

CHICKEN

CHICKEN

CHEESE

CHEESE

BREAD

BREAD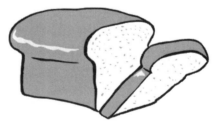

NUTS

SNACK

SNACK

JUNK FOOD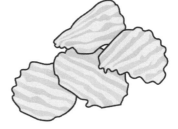

JUNK FOOD

FAST FOOD

FAST FOOD

MALCOLM AND THE PURPLE TIE

APPETIZER

OPPOSITIONAL ORANGE SQUARES

Appetizer Ingredients:

Master Chef:
- ☐ Orange construction paper
- ☐ Green construction paper
- ☐ Markers
- ☐ Scissors

Student Chefs: (4 or more players—even number)
- ✗ No materials required

Appetizer Preparation:

Cut the orange and green construction paper into squares. Write one word on an orange square and its antonym on a green square. Suggested antonyms are:

in	out
yes	no
up	down
left	right
good	bad

Make enough orange and green squares so each child can have a square.

Appetizer Activity:

Give each child an orange square or a matching green square. Then introduce the activity by saying:

An *antonym* is a word that is the opposite of another word such as, listen/ignore. Each of you has either an orange square or a green square. Your task is to find the person who has a match for your square. If you have an orange square, you are looking for a person with a green square. If you have a green square, you are looking for a person who has an orange square.

When you find your match, the two of you must make one silly sentence that includes your antonyms. Then each pair will act out its silly sentence for the rest of us. Have fun!

Begin the activity.

"AGREE WITH ME" QUICHE-A-LA-KING

Main Course Ingredients:

Master Chef:
- [ ] Chalkboard and chalk
- [ ] *Malcolm And The Purple Tie* story (pages 119-121)

Student Chefs:
- ✗ No materials required

Main Course Preparation:

None required.

Main Course Activity:

Read the following story aloud. Pause at the involvement questions for the children's answers.

Malcolm And The Purple Tie

The Engelton family was a proud family. Each morning, Mr. Engelton and his son Malcolm dressed in:

their fine dark slacks,

their crisp white shirts,

their fancy braided belts,

their soft felt hats,

and their distinguished purple ties.

Mr. Engelton ALWAYS wore his purple tie, as had his father before him. "Purple," Mr. Engelton said proudly, "is the color of royalty and distinction. Why, there is not an Engelton alive who would wear any color tie, except purple," he boasted.

STOP Ask the children to describe the Engelton family.

After Mr. Engelton and Malcolm donned their fancy clothes, they strolled down the streets and throughout the town.

Everyone in the town respected the Engelton family and was happy that the Engeltons were citizens of this fine town. But what the townspeople especially admired about the Engeltons were their fancy clothes and, most especially, their distinguished purple ties.

"Purple is a sign of royalty and distinction," they all whispered and nodded as Malcolm and his dad greeted them while passing.

After their stroll, Mr. Engelton and Malcolm would join the others in the park to sip tea and talk of faraway countries in faraway lands.

In the evening, everyone would gather in the town square to discuss the events of the day and enjoy a delicious gourmet meal.

Malcolm and his family always sat in the center. The townspeople would have it no other way. When the Engeltons sat in the center everyone could enjoy the delicious meal while admiring the Engelton's fancy clothes.

STOP Ask the children: "How did the townspeople feel about the Engeltons?"

After years of doing things the same way day after day and year after year, Malcolm decided it was time for a change.

So when Mr. Engelton and Malcolm donned their fancy clothes and strolled down the street and throughout the town the next morning, things were very different.

The Engelton family smiled proudly that morning, but no one smiled back.

The Engelton family nodded, but no one nodded in return.

Mr. Engelton announced proudly that purple was the color of royalty and distinction, but no one agreed.

The townspeople just whispered and pointed as the Engeltons passed by.

STOP Ask the children: "What do you think the problem is?"

"What on earth could this mean?" Mr. Engelton asked Malcolm. "They have always admired our fine dark slacks, our crisp white shirts, our fancy braided belts, our soft felt hats, and our distinguished purple … our distinguished purple … Malcolm, where is your distinguished purple tie?" Mr. Engelton asked as his regal face turned beet red.

"How could you forget to wear something so important?" asked Mr. Engelton.

"I did not forget to wear it," answered Malcolm. "I just decided that maybe this red tie would look better with our felt hats."

STOP Ask the children: "Was Malcolm trying to upset his dad?"

That afternoon, Mr. Engelton talked with Malcolm and reminded him of the importance of the purple ties. "Purple is a sign of royalty and distinction. Engeltons ALWAYS wear purple ties, Malcolm."

When Mr. Engelton and Malcolm walked down the street and strolled through the town the next morning, the townspeople still pointed and whispered.

"What on earth could this mean?" asked Mr. Engelton.

When Mr. Engelton looked at Malcolm this time, he saw that his son *was* wearing his distinguished purple tie. He was also wearing his soft felt hat, his braided belt, and his dark slacks. But he was not wearing his crisp white shirt. He was wearing a blue shirt with red polka dots!

Mr. Engelton smiled a very uncomfortable smile and hurried Malcolm away from the busy streets and the pointing and whispering townspeople.

STOP Ask the children: "How did Mr. Engelton feel? How do you think Malcolm felt?"

When Mr. Engelton and Malcolm strolled through the town the next day, the townspeople still pointed and whispered. This time, they even hid their faces.

"What on earth could this mean?" asked Mr. Engelton, growing very frustrated.

Malcolm was wearing his purple tie, his crisp white shirt, his soft felt hat, and his dark slacks. But he was wearing Mr. Engelton's dark slacks and he was not wearing his special braided belt.

Malcolm's oversized pants hung below his waist! "Malcolm," whispered Mr. Engelton in a hushed and very anxious voice, "Where is your belt? And what happened to your pants?"

Mr. Engelton and Malcolm did not finish their stroll.

STOP Ask the children: "What do you think will happen next?"

"Malcolm," asked Mr. Engelton, "are you not proud to be an Engelton?"

"I am proud to be an Engelton, Dad," answered Malcolm, "but I am also proud to be just Malcolm. "If we changed things around just a little, I would be even more proud to be an Engelton. And I can do it without making the townspeople point and whisper."

So Mr. Engelton and Malcolm worked out an agreement. And when everyone met in the square the next evening to discuss the events of the day and enjoy a delicious gourmet meal, Malcolm asked if he could speak to all the townspeople about the Engelton's fine dark slacks, their crisp white shirts, their fancy braided belts, their soft felt hats, and their distinguished purple ties.

When Malcolm finished his speech, everyone applauded. His mom and dad had never been more proud of him than they were at that very moment.

So the next morning, Mr. Engelton and Malcolm donned their fancy clothes and proudly strolled down the street and throughout the town.

Mr. Engelton was dressed in his fine dark slacks.

Malcolm was dressed in his fine slacks, but they were not dark.

Mr. Engelton was dressed in his crisp white shirt.

Malcolm was dressed in his crisp shirt, but it was not white.

Mr. Engelton wore his soft felt hat.

Malcolm wore a fine hat, but it was not felt.

Mr. Engelton wore his braided belt.

Malcolm wore his belt, but it was not braided.

Mr. Engelton wore his distinguished purple tie.

And Malcolm wore his distinguished purple tie.

"Dad," said Malcolm as he nodded proudly at the adoring townspeople, "no Engelton should ever be caught without his distinguished purple tie. Right, Dad?"

"That's right, son," said Mr. Engelton proudly. "That's right."

FINISH the story by asking the children: "How did Malcolm and Mr. Engelton solve the problem?"

DUELING DIFFERENCES DRAMA BARS

Dessert Ingredients:

Master Chef:
☐ Copy of *Dueling Drama Situation Sheet* (page 123)
☐ Index cards
☐ Table

Student Chefs: (2 or more players—students will work in pairs)
✗ No materials required

Dessert Preparation:

Number the index cards the following way:

1A on the front of one card

1B on the front of the next card

2A on the front of the next card

2B on the front of the next card and so on until you have numbered cards equal to the number of students participating.

Dessert Activity:

Lay the cards face-down on the table and mix them up. Then say:

Come to the table and select one card. When everyone has a card, find your partner by matching your number with another child's number. For example, if you draw a card that says 1A, you will look for the person who has the card numbered 2A. That person will be your partner.

Have the children take their cards and find their partners. Then continue:

I am going to assign each of you a situation. Each of the situations contains a conflict. After everyone has a situation, I will give you a few minutes to decide what could be a peaceful solution for the conflict and how you will enact the situation and the solution. When you do your role-play, the child with the A card will be the adult or oldest person. The person with the B card will be the child.

Read the situations from the *Dueling Drama Situation Sheet*, make the assignments, and tell the children how much time they have to prepare their role-plays. Then have each pair enact its situation.

DUELING DRAMA SITUATION SHEET

(Choose one of the following for each pair of students.)

Each pair of children must find a peaceful solution to their assigned situations. The children must then role-play the conflict and its solution for the group.

1. You like loud music; your parent hates loud music.

2. Your room is messy; your parent wants you to keep it clean.

3. Your teacher thinks homework is important; you think homework is boring.

4. Your parent want you to exercise; you would rather play videogames.

5. Your grandparent wants you to help with the chores; you would rather ride your dirt bike.

6. You want to dye your hair green; your parent won't allow it.

7. Your parent wants you to eat a salad for lunch; you want to eat a burger and fries.

8. Your curfew is 8:00; you want to come in at 10:00.

9. Your teacher wants you to make good grades; you think good grades are for geeks.

10. Your parent tells you to wash up for dinner; you want to eat first and wash up later.

11. Your parent tells you not to leave your room without permission; you want to visit your friends

12. Your older sibling wants to swim laps with you in the evenings after school; you want to watch your favorite TV program in the evenings.

13. Your allowance is $5.00 per week; you want $10.00 per week.

14. Your parent expects you to use polite words like *please* and *thank you*; you see no purpose in using polite words.

THE MUGAROTS

APPETIZER

TEMPTING TREASURE TREATS

Appetizer Ingredients:

Master Chef:
- ☐ Copy of *Directive Cards* (page 131)
- ☐ Gift bag
- ☐ Small, inexpensive gifts
- ☐ Marker
- ☐ Scissors
- ☐ Small box or other container
- ☐ Chalk or masking tape

Student Chefs: (2 or more players)
- ✗ No materials required

Appetizer Preparation:

Purchase some small, inexpensive gifts and place them in a gift bag labeled *Treasure Bag.* Make a copy of the *Directive Cards*, cut them apart, and place them in a box. Mark the line with chalk or masking tape where the students are to begin the game. This should be about 15 feet from the *Treasure Bag,* which is the finish line.

TAKE 1 STEP FORWARD

Appetizer Activity:

Divide the students into two equal groups. Then introduce the activity by saying:

I will chose one child to play from each group. Whoever is chosen will begin at the starting point. Your task is to reach the *Treasure Bag,* and you will do that by drawing cards from this box. Each card will tell you to either move toward or away from the *Treasure Bag.* After you have read the card, return it to the box, then move as the card indicates. You may forfeit your turn by saying *Pass* before drawing a card from the box. The other player will then draw a card. The two players will continue taking turns drawing cards until one player reaches the *Treasure Bag* and wins the game for his or her group. Those players will then stand aside, and I will chose another child from each group to play. When everyone has had a chance to play, the winners from each round will play a final game to see who will get to keep the *Treasure Bag.*

Begin the game.

(**Note:** The game may be modified for larger groups by choosing several children from each group to play at the same time. Have each child select a card. Then have each child read his/her card aloud and move as directed. Place all the cards back in the box and continue playing until one player reaches the finish line.)

GREEN AND GROOVY GARDEN GOULASH

Main Course Ingredients:

Master Chef:
☐ *The Mugarots* story (pages 125-129)

Student Chefs:
☐ Drawing paper
☐ Crayons or markers

Main Course Preparation:

None required.

Main Course Activity:

Distribute drawing paper and crayons or markers to the children. Then read the following story aloud. Pause at the involvement questions for the children's answers.

The Mugarots

Each day, the Mugarots ate delicious croittles from the magical garden and drank sparkling water from the crystal stream on the east side of the village.

The Mugarots loved their lovely garden and worked hard to keep it beautiful and tidy.

They used special tools to till and smooth the dark, rich soil. Then they sprinkled the garden with cool water that flowed from the crystal stream.

Afterward, the Mugarots stood and watched proudly as the warm, golden sun gave rich color to the croittles that grew in the garden.

In the evening, the strong Mugarots gently pulled the colorful croittles from the thick woven vines, diced them, and tossed them in with the dark green leaves.

STOP Ask the children: "What are *croittles*?"

The Mugarots ate and laughed. Then they laughed and ate. They ate and ate until their bellies were full! When they were full, they stopped eating. The Mugarots never ate more than they needed.

After they ate, they played games and ran about the village jumping over thick bushes, climbing the big rocks, and skipping through the tall grasses. All of the Mugarots, that is, except Myrtle!

STOP Ask the children: "Why do you think Myrtle would not run, climb, or skip?"

Myrtle tried to skip, but she always fell down. She tried climbing big rocks, but they crumbled to pieces. She tried jumping the bushes, but caused such a rumble that the others begged her to stop.

Myrtle could not skip, climb, or jump because she ate bolups and they made her plump!

But things had not always been that way.

Myrtle was once the happiest and leanest Mugarot in the entire village. Eating croittles and drinking the crystal water kept her that way.

Myrtle and every Mugarot in the village knew that eating bolups from the west side of the village was something no Mugarot should ever do!

STOP Ask the children: "What do you think *bolups* are?"

So each day, all day long, the Mugarots reminded each other …

"Eat your croittles and stay away from bolups. Eat your croittles and stay away from bolups."

They sang it while working in the garden.

They whispered it while standing in the golden sun.

And they shouted it while skipping through the tall grasses.

No Mugarot from the village had ever eaten a bolup and neither had any Mugarot before them. For they knew that eating just one bolup would cause something awful to happen.

No Mugarot, that is, until the day Myrtle the Mugarot got curious.

STOP Ask the children: "What do you think Myrtle is going to do?"

While Myrtle was working one day she began to think about bolups. Try as she might, she could not stop. This happened day after day. She even dreamed about bolups. "Are they sweet or sour? Are they crunchy or chewy? I must know," she said out loud.

The next day, while the other Mugarots watched the warm sun bathe the colorful croittles, Myrtle quietly slipped away to the west side of the village.

She could smell the bolups even before she reached the patch. "Sweet and chewy," she said with excitement. "I bet they are sweet and chewy."

Finally, she reached the patch. It was not pretty and green like the garden, but Myrtle had never seen or smelled anything so delightful and friendly.

At that moment, something deep inside her told her not to touch the bolups. She wanted to walk away, but the smell of the bolups made her stay.

STOP Ask the children: "What do you think Myrtle should do?"

She tore a fat bolup from the patch and held it in her slender hand. She placed it to her nose and took a long, deep whiff. "How delightful!" she said. Then she closed her eyes and slowly opened her mouth and took a big bite of the juicy bolup.

"Ummm," she said.

Myrtle had never tasted anything so delicious! She ate and ate until she was tired. Then she fell asleep.

STOP Ask the children: "Why did she fall asleep? Do you fall asleep after you eat?"

Later that evening, after eating the delicious croittles and green leaves, the other Mugarots began to look for Myrtle. They checked the thick bushes. She was not there. They checked the big rock, but she was not there. They checked the tall grasses, but Myrtle was not there, either.

The Mugarots searched the entire village for Myrtle. When they found her near the patch on the west side of the village, they knew something was wrong.

"Myrtle!" they exclaimed when they found her. "The bolups! You ate bolups!"

"I did no such thing," denied Myrtle.

"Myrtle, look at you!" they cried in horror. "You are three times the size you were this morning!"

"No need to worry," said Myrtle. "I will just wear bigger clothing."

But there was plenty to worry about. As they walked back to the village, Myrtle could not walk as fast as the others. She had to stop often to catch her breath. The others worried, but Myrtle thought only of the delicious taste of the bolups.

Seeing the state Myrtle was in, the other Mugarots knew that they needed to do something. "We must get you to the Great Yakaron," they exclaimed. "He will know what to do."

STOP Ask the children: "Who do you think the Great Yakaron is?"

The Great Yakaron explained the legend that once you have eaten the bolups, you can think of nothing else. Eating bolups will make you larger and larger and rob you of the things that make you happy. The bolups will steal your desire to eat croittles and drink the water from the crystal stream. Red spots will cover the face and body of a Mugarot who stops eating croittles. When this happens, the poor Mugarot has no choice but to leave the village.

As the Great Yakaron spoke, the others trembled with fear. Myrtle trembled because she wanted bolups.

STOP Ask the children: "Why did the Mugarots tremble when the Great Yakaron spoke?"

The next day, Myrtle's friends again found her asleep near the bolup patch. "Come, Myrtle, we must take you away."

"No," said Myrtle breathing deeply, "leave me. I have to have more delicious bolups."

No matter how hard they tried, the Mugarots could not make Myrtle move. She had grown too heavy.

Day after day, Myrtle found her way to the bolups. Day after day, she grew more and more plump. Everyone wanted to help, but no one knew how. It seemed nothing could stop Myrtle from eating bolups.

They tried tying her up, but she always broke free.

They tried blindfolding her, but she still found her way.

They tried hiding the patch, but she sniffed it right out.

Myrtle grew bigger and bigger and BIGGER!

Myrtle had become very sad, for she realized that what she had done was very foolish. She also realized that she could not stop herself.

The sadder she became, the more bolups she ate. The more bolups she ate, the bigger she got!

The villagers had never seen such a plump Mugarot, and they began to stare. Some giggled. Others even gave unfriendly looks.

STOP Ask the children: "How do you think this made Myrtle feel?"

Myrtle wanted to stop eating bolups, but she could not.

Each day, Myrtle went to the bolup patch. Sometimes days would go by before she waddled back to the village.

After Myrtle had eaten the bolups one day, big red spots covered her face. The spots were as colorful as some of the red croittles Myrtle had once eaten with the villagers.

Myrtle became frightened. "What is this?" she cried.

A couple of wise Mugarots answered, "They are *pomplets*, Myrtle. The pomplets appear on Mugarots who no longer eat croittles. Soon they will cover your entire body. Then you can no longer live in the village."

Hearing this, Myrtle remembered the warning of the Great Yakaron.

STOP Ask the children to use their paper and crayons/markers to draw a picture of what they believe Myrtle looked like.

Myrtle began to feel even sadder.

"I've got to do something," she said. But she did nothing but eat bolups.

Soon Myrtle grew so plump and so weak she could hardly move. Her friends did not know what to do. They did not know how to help. But a very strong and very brave Mugarot from a nearby village saw Myrtle and knew exactly what to do.

This Mugarot went back to his village. When he returned, he had a tiny bottle and a big smile.

"Take a sniff," he said politely, placing the bottle next to Myrtle's nose.

"Who are you?" asked Myrtle. "And what is in that bottle?"

"Take a sniff," he said again. "This will help you get to the crystal stream. After you reach the stream, you must take a drink. There you will find your strength."

STOP Ask the children: "Do you think this Mugarot is trying to help or trick Myrtle?"

Myrtle sniffed from the bottle and waddled to the stream. She leaned forward to drink and saw a very sad, very enormous Mugarot with red spots all over her face.

"What have I done?" she cried.

The Mugarot began to smile, for he knew that the crystal stream and his kind words would help Myrtle.

"I cannot stop eating bolups," admitted Myrtle.

"In time, you will," he spoke softly. "I will help you. The first thing we must do is get rid of the pomplets. To do so, you must sprinkle your face with cool water from the stream and allow the warm sun to dry it. Then rub bitter croittles all over your face. Do this for seven days. Then I shall return."

Myrtle did everything the kind Mugarot had instructed her to do. After seven days, the pomplets were gone.

STOP Ask the children: "How do you feel about the kind Mugarot now?"

But Myrtle still craved bolups.

When the kind Mugarot returned, he told Myrtle the only way to keep the pomplets from coming back was to start eating croittles again.

"I will try," said Myrtle.

"You can," insisted the kind Mugarot. "You must."

Myrtle tried, but it was not easy. Eating bolups had taken her taste for croittles away.

Myrtle still wanted to eat bolups. But each day she ate more and more croittles and began to sip water from the crystal stream. After a while, eating croittles was just as easy as eating bolups.

STOP Ask the children: "How do you think Myrtle is feeling?"

After many weeks of eating croittles and the stranger's kind words, Myrtle began to feel happy again. The other Mugarots saw this and they were happy, too. They asked Myrtle to play with them and ran together about the village jumping over thick bushes, climbing the big rocks, and skipping through tall grasses.

The stranger's medicine had worked.

In time, the power of the bolups faded away. When Myrtle drank from the crystal stream, she saw that she was strong again and very lean. Myrtle could not wait to thank the kind stranger, but he had disappeared.

STOP Ask the children: "Where do you think the kind stranger went?"

One evening, Myrtle found the stranger eating croittles with the other Mugarots. "Kind stranger," she asked, "why is it that you took the time to help me?"

The stranger replied, "My mother was once curious like you, Myrtle. She ate bolups and became very ill, very tired, very plump, and very sad. A kind and gentle Mugarot from another village gave her a dose of the same medicine I gave you. It is the code of the Mugarots that once you have beaten the bolups, you have a duty to others."

"What was the magic potion in the bottle that helped me?" asked Myrtle.

"Confidence," replied the kind stranger. "It was a simple dose of confidence."

As the proud Mugarots worked in the garden the next day and watched the sun rise, Myrtle saw a curious, young, and very lean Mugarot sneaking out to the west side of the village.

Because of the kind Mugarot who had helped her, Myrtle knew just what to do.

FINISH the story by asking the children: "What do you think Myrtle will do?"

HELEN'S HEALTH FRUIT SQUARES

Dessert Ingredients:

Master Chef:
- ☐ Several colors of brightly colored construction paper
- ☐ Dark green construction paper

Student Chefs:
- ☐ Paper plate
- ☐ Gluestick

Dessert Preparation:

Obtain paper plates and a gluestick for each child. Set out several stacks of brightly colored construction paper and dark green construction paper.

Dessert Activity:

Distribute a paper plate and a gluestick to each student. Then introduce the activity by saying:

The Mugarots ate fresh, colorful foods that grew in their beautiful garden. You may select different colors of construction paper and tear them into shapes to make croittles and use dark green construction paper to make leaves. When you have enough for your meal, glue the torn croittles and leaves onto the paper plate to make a beautiful and delicious Mugarot meal. When everyone has finished, we will share our meals. Then you can discuss how each croittle you chose crunches, squishes, or squirts when eaten. You may then take your Mugarot meal home and share it with your family.

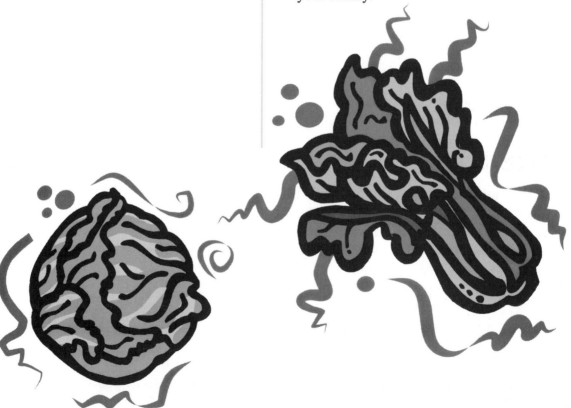

TAKE 1 STEP FORWARD

GUIDANCE FOR THE GOURMET DIRECTIVE CARDS
© 2006 MAR⋆CO PRODUCTS, INC. 1-800-448-2197

TAKE 1 STEP BACKWARD

GUIDANCE FOR THE GOURMET DIRECTIVE CARDS
© 2006 MAR⋆CO PRODUCTS, INC. 1-800-448-2197

TAKE 2 STEPS FORWARD

GUIDANCE FOR THE GOURMET DIRECTIVE CARDS
© 2006 MAR⋆CO PRODUCTS, INC. 1-800-448-2197

TAKE 2 STEPS BACKWARD

GUIDANCE FOR THE GOURMET DIRECTIVE CARDS
© 2006 MAR⋆CO PRODUCTS, INC. 1-800-448-2197

TAKE 3 STEPS FORWARD

GUIDANCE FOR THE GOURMET DIRECTIVE CARDS
© 2006 MAR⋆CO PRODUCTS, INC. 1-800-448-2197

TAKE 3 STEPS BACKWARD

GUIDANCE FOR THE GOURMET DIRECTIVE CARDS
© 2006 MAR⋆CO PRODUCTS, INC. 1-800-448-2197

CHOOSE A PLAYER TO GO BACK TO THE STARTING LINE

GUIDANCE FOR THE GOURMET DIRECTIVE CARDS
© 2006 MAR⋆CO PRODUCTS, INC. 1-800-448-2197

GO BACK TO THE STARTING LINE

GUIDANCE FOR THE GOURMET DIRECTIVE CARDS
© 2006 MAR⋆CO PRODUCTS, INC. 1-800-448-2197

GIVE UP YOUR TURN

GUIDANCE FOR THE GOURMET DIRECTIVE CARDS
© 2006 MAR⋆CO PRODUCTS, INC. 1-800-448-2197

GIVE UP YOUR TURN

GUIDANCE FOR THE GOURMET DIRECTIVE CARDS
© 2006 MAR⋆CO PRODUCTS, INC. 1-800-448-2197

THE SAPLING

APPETIZER

JEALOUS JUBILEE

Appetizer Ingredients:

Master Chef:
☐ Fancy box

Student Chefs: (2 or more players)
✗ No materials required

Appetizer Preparation:

Obtain a box. If it is not very attractive, decorate it.

Appetizer Activity:

Introduce the activity by saying:

I will choose one person to be Jess and another student to be Jody. Jess will hide Jody's beautiful box while Jody is out of the room. Jess will do this because he or she is jealous that Jody has such a beautiful box. When Jody returns to the room, he or she will want to find the box. All of you will know where the box is hidden, but you may only direct Jody by saying "hot" if he or she is going in the right direction, or "cold" if he or she is going in the wrong direction. With different people yelling "hot" or "cold," it may be difficult for Jody to find the box. But if Jody finds the box within 15 seconds, Jody will become Jess. Then I will choose a new Jody and Jess will hide the box again. We will continue the game until everyone has had a chance to be Jealous Jess or we run out of time.

Begin the game.

ENVY-FREE EGG FRITTERS

Main Course Ingredients:

Master Chef:
- [ ] *The Sapling* story (pages 133-135)

Student Chefs:
- ✗ No materials required

Main Course Preparation:

None required.

Main Course Activity:

Read the following story aloud. Pause at the involvement questions for the children's answers.

The Sapling

There once was a little sapling that grew at his mother's side. The rain bathed his tiny trunk. The sunlight kissed his tender leaves, and his mother's gentle words nourished his roots.

"You are a fine little sapling," his mom would say. "You will grow tall and strong. You will be happy, and you will make others happy."

STOP Ask the children: "What is a *sapling*?"

Each day as the rain bathed his trunk, the sunlight kissed his leaves, and his mom's words nourished his roots, the little sapling grew.

The sapling grew and grew until he had grown into a fine young tree.

He was tall. He was strong. He was happy, and he made his mother happy.

Since the young tree was no longer a sapling, it was time for him to leave his mother's side. So the fine young tree made his new home in a beautiful park near the village at the edge of the town.

The rain bathed his sturdy trunk. The sunlight kissed his broad green leaves, and he grew taller and stronger.

What a fine young tree he was!

The children loved this young tree better than any of the other trees in the park. His strong branches made them happy, and their happy voices nourished his roots.

STOP Ask the children: "Why did the children love the tree so much?"

The other trees in the park did not like the fine young tree. For the children who had once climbed their branches now climbed his branches. And the happy voices that once nourished their roots now nourished the roots of the fine young tree.

While the fine young tree waited for the children each morning, he stood tall and stretched his big, strong branches. He then used his broad green leaves to stroke his sturdy trunk.

The other trees watched as he stood tall. They watched as he stretched his big, strong branches. And they watched as he used his broad green leaves to stroke his sturdy trunk.

Then the unfriendly trees spoke to the fine young tree.

"You are not so tall. You are not so strong. You are not such a fine young tree, and you do not make us happy."

STOP Ask the children: "Why are the trees so unfriendly?"

The young tree had never heard such angry and unkind words. But he still stood tall and stretched his big, strong branches. And he used his broad green leaves to stroke his sturdy trunk.

Then the children came. His strong branches made them happy, and their happy voices nourished his roots.

The next morning the unfriendly trees watched him stretch as they had done the day before. They spoke the same angry, unkind words.

"You are not so tall. You are not so strong. You are not such a fine young tree, and you do not make us happy."

The angry and unkind words felt more unfriendly than they had felt the day before. And …

The young tree did not stand so tall. He did not feel so strong. But he was such a fine tree, he still made the children happy. And their happy voices nourished his roots.

STOP Ask the children: "Did the unfriendly words hurt the young tree?"

Day after day after day, the unfriendly trees spoke the same angry, unkind words to the young tree. Soon he did not feel like such a fine tree. And he did not look like a fine tree.

He did not stand tall. He did not feel strong. He lost his broad leaves, and his branches seemed broken.

The young tree did not make the children happy. Their happy voices did not nourish his roots.

Since the young tree no longer made the children happy, he would soon be moved from the park. The young tree did not want to be moved. He loved the beautiful park and he loved the happy children. He even loved the unfriendly trees, though he did not like their unkind words.

STOP Ask the children: "Why are the unfriendly trees so mean?"

That night, as the young tree slept, a cool, gentle breeze softly soothed him with its sweet, refreshing scent. It was the same scent the young tree had known as a sapling.

Then the gentle breeze whispered to the young tree:

"You are a fine young tree. You are tall. You are strong. You will be happy, and you will make others happy."

STOP Ask the children: "What did the gentle breeze do?"

When the young tree awoke the next morning, his branches no longer seemed broken. And he had grown new green leaves.

The young tree stood tall and felt strong. The rain bathed his sturdy trunk. The sunlight kissed his new green leaves, and he was a fine young tree.

The unfriendly trees were astonished when they saw the young tree.

STOP Ask the children: "Why were the unfriendly trees surprised?"

They watched him stand tall. They watched him stretch his big, strong branches, and they watched him use his new green leaves to stroke his sturdy trunk.

Then the unfriendly trees spoke to the fine young tree:

"You are not so tall. You are not so strong. You are not such a fine young tree, and you do not make us happy."

This time, the angry, unkind words did not hurt the young tree. And the fine young tree quietly spoke to the unfriendly trees:

"But you are tall," he said. "And you are strong.

"You have broad green leaves and big, strong branches. You make the park beautiful and you make the children happy."

When the unfriendly trees heard the kind words of the fine young tree, they were sorry for their unkind words. For they knew now that this fine young tree was a special tree indeed.

STOP Ask the children: "How did the unfriendly trees feel now?"

The next morning, when the fine young tree stood tall, stretched his big, strong, branches, and used his broad green leaves to stroke his sturdy trunk; the unfriendly trees also stood tall. They stretched their big, strong, branches and used their broad green leaves to stroke their sturdy trunks. And …

The unfriendly trees were no longer unfriendly. The unfriendly trees were now happy trees. Because the kind words of the fine young tree made them happy and nourished their roots.

JEALOUS GELATIN JINGLES

Dessert Ingredients:

Master Chef:
- ☐ Copy of *Musical Strips* (page 137—optional)
- ☐ Bag (optional)
- ☐ Pencil (optional)

Student Chefs:
- ☐ Paper-towel roll
- ☐ Hole-punch
- ☐ Yarn
- ☐ Jingle bells

Dessert Preparation:

Following the activity directions, make a sample instrument. To give the children more opportunities to use their instruments, you may add this optional activity. Make a copy of the *Musical Strips* and cut them apart. Add any other types of music you would like on the blank strips. Put the strips in the bag to use it at the end of the activity.

Dessert Activity:

Distribute paper-towel rolls, yarn, hole-punches, and small jingle bells to each child. Then say:

Today, we are going to make jingle bell instruments. Then we are going to use the instruments to play different styles of music. Punch four holes around the bottom of the paper-towel roll and four holes around the top of the paper-towel roll. (*Show the children your sample and pause for them to complete the task.*) Thread the yarn through the punched holes and tie the jingle bells onto the yarn. (*Show the children your sample and pause for them to complete the task.*)

Begin by having the children play this jingle slowly.

"You are not so tall," they said.

"And you are not so strong.

You are not such a fine young tree,

and you do not make us happy."

Then have the children play this jingle with lots of pizzazz!

"But you are tall," he said.

"And you are strong.

You have broad green leaves and big strong, branches.

You make the park beautiful, and you make the children happy."

(***Note:*** If you are using the bag with the different music styles, have the children use their instruments to play the type of music written on the strip of paper they pull from the bag. Continue the game until all of the strips have been drawn from the bag.)

 COUNTRY

RAP

 OPERA

ROCK

 JAZZ

HIP HOP

MAD GEORGE

APPETIZER

HOPPIN' MAD MUFFINS

Appetizer Ingredients:

Master Chef:
- ☐ *Hoppin' Mad Cards* (pages 142-145)
- ☐ Card stock
- ☐ Paper for bunny hats (optional)
- ☐ Chalk or masking tape

Student Chefs: (2 or more players)
- ✗ No materials required

Appetizer Preparation:

Reproduce the cards on card stock, cut them out, and stack them. There are extra blank cards you may use if you would like the children to add more suggestions. If the children are at an age where bunny hats would add to the activity, you may make—or have the children make—bunny hats. To make a bunny hat, fit a strip of paper around each child's head and staple the ends together. Attach bunny ears. This should be done before the session begins. Mark a finish line on the floor with masking tape or chalk.

> You get a mean note, and you write one back.

Appetizer Activity:

Have the children line up across the back of the room. Then introduce the activity by saying:

> This is my stack of *Hoppin' Mad Cards*. I will go from one of you to the other, pulling a card from the stack, and reading it aloud. The cards describe different situations. You must decide whether the situation described on the card would be a wise choice or an unwise choice. When it is your turn, if I pull a card that describes a wise choice, all of your classmates will shout, "Hop, hop, hop, little bunny!" *(For older children, you may wish to change the text.)* The player will then hop three spaces toward the finish line. *(Point to the finish line.)* But if I choose a card that describes an unwise choice, you must shout, "Hoppin' mad!" That player may not move forward. The first person to hop over the finish line is the winner.

Begin the game by drawing a card. After reading the card, place it back in the stack, but not necessarily on the bottom.

(***Note:*** Be prepared to explain why a choice is wise or unwise if the children seem uncertain.)

FURIOUSLY FLAMING FISH FLORENTINE

Main Course Ingredients:

Master Chef:
- [ ] *Mad George* story (pages 139-140)

Student Chefs:
- ✗ No materials required

Main Course Preparation:

None required.

Main Course Activity:

Read the following story aloud. Pause at the involvement questions for the children's answers.

Mad George

George was always mad.

He got mad at the sun because it was too bright. But he put on his sunglasses, and that made things all right.

He got mad at the moon because it was too round. "Why can't the moon be a triangle?" he groaned.

He got mad at the rain because it made him wet. Then he opened his umbrella and that kept him dry.

George was always mad.

STOP Ask the children: "Do you know anyone like George?"

He got mad at his brother for wearing his new baseball shirt. So George wore his brother's new baseball cap and that made him feel better.

He got mad when it was his turn to take out the trash. "I hate taking out the trash. It smells!" he complained.

He got mad when his mom fixed zucchini for dinner. "I hate zucchini!" yelled George. Then he fed it to the dog.

George was always mad.

He got mad on the bus when the seats were all taken.

He got mad during lunch because no pizza was left.

He got mad during class when he couldn't spell *banana*.

STOP Ask the children: "Have you ever felt like George?"

George was always mad. He got mad during recess when he had to play *chase*.

He got mad at his hamster for running away.

He got mad when he fell and ripped his pants and everyone laughed.

George was always mad!

He got mad at his own birthday party, because it was a surprise. "I hate surprises," he grumbled.

He got mad when Andy called him a name. George punched Andy in the arm.

"George," asked his teacher, "why are you always so mad?"

Mom and Dad talked with George. "George," they said, "getting mad sometimes is OK, but getting mad all the time is not OK. And hurting others when you are mad is not OK, George! Feeling mad is not the only way to feel."

STOP Ask the children: "What are some other ways to feel?"

"It's OK to feel sad if your pet hamster runs away," Mom and Dad continued. "It's even OK not to like surprises, but it is not OK to always feel mad."

"There are things you can do so you won't feel so mad," said Mom. "You can play with your new hamster, listen to music, or sing a song. Or what about riding your bike, helping a neighbor, or eating an ice cream cone?"

"George," said Dad, "I'm going to tell you what my father told me to help take my mad feelings away."

STOP Ask the children: "Who is trying to help George?"

Dad began:

"There once was a fish
that stayed mad all the day,
so small, yet so grumpy,
he chased others away.

"He swam all alone,
never smiled … never glad.
Not one single friend
did this grouchy fish have.

"One day, he got lonely.
There was no one around.
He drifted away
and, in sorrow, did drown."

George listened. He did not get mad.

STOP Ask the children: "What do you think George was thinking?"

The next day, George smiled at the sun, winked at the moon, and danced in the rain.

He played with his brother.

He took out the trash.

He ate all his zucchini.

He even learned to spell *banana*.

When George fell down and ripped his pants during recess, and all the kids laughed. George did not get mad. George laughed, too.

George learned not to feel mad all the time.

George wanted to have friends.

George wanted to be happy.

George did not want to be lonely like the fish.

And so George decided not to always feel mad.

He decided to be happy.

FINISH the story by asking the children:

"Did George change? Why?"

"Is it OK to get mad?"

"Is it OK to be mad all the time? Why?"

DELECTABLE MAD-BUSTER SCROLLS

Dessert Ingredients:

Master Chef:
- ☐ *Mad-Busters* list (page 146)
- ☐ Decorative computer paper or blank paper
- ☐ Computer (optional)

Student Chefs:
- ☐ Ribbon or yarn
- ☐ Copy of *Mad-Busters* list (optional—page 146)
- ☐ Crayons or markers (optional)
- ☐ Glitter (optional)
- ☐ Gluestick (optional)

Dessert Preparation:

You can perform this activity in one of three ways:

1. On the computer, type the *Mad-Busters* list so it can be printed on a sheet of decorative computer paper. Have the children go to the computer and print off their list. Then have them roll their paper into a scroll and tie a piece of ribbon or yarn around it.

2. If decorative computer paper is not available, type the *Mad-Busters* list on the computer. Print a copy of the list for each child on standard white paper. The children can decorate their paper with crayons or markers. Glitter could also be added to some areas using a gluestick. Then have them roll their paper into a scroll and tie a piece of ribbon or yarn around it.

3. Make a copy of the *Mad-Busters* list for each child. Have the children decorate their paper with crayons or markers. Glitter could also be added to some areas using a gluestick. Then have them roll their paper into a scroll and tie a piece of ribbon or yarn around it.

Dessert Activity:

Decide which way you want to perform the activity. Then explain it to the children.

You are mad at your teacher, but you talk about your feelings with him or her.

You get a mean note, and you write one back.

You get teased, and you ignore it.

Your money was stolen, and you tell the teacher.

You got pushed, and you wait for an apology.

You can't do your homework, so you ask for help.

Someone called you "stupid," and you walked away.

A friend broke your toy, and you stayed calm.

Someone teased you, and you ignored him or her.

You are angry, but you don't fight.

Your brother hogs the TV, so you read a book.

You are angry, and you punch a pillow.

You are angry, but you stop and think.

Someone is rude to you, and you take a deep breath.

Someone rips your notebook, and you stay calm.

Mom says "no" to ice cream, and you eat an apple.

You get a mean note, and you throw it away.

Others tease you, and you laugh with them.

You get teased, and you start a fight.

Your pencil was stolen, and you punched the person you think took it.

Someone lied about you,
so you told a lie about
him or her.

You got pushed, and
you pushed back.

You can't do your
homework, so you
forget about it.

You got punched, and
you punched back.

A friend broke your toy,
so you ripped
his or her book.

You stole a pair of shoes
because you hated yours.

You are angry, and
you get into a fight.

You would not share
the TV with your brother.

You are mad at your
teacher, so you shout
at him or her.

You get angry, and
kick the desk over.

You do not stop and think when you are angry.

Someone is rude to you, so you are rude back.

Someone rips your notebook, and you rip his or hers.

Mom says "no," but you don't listen.

MAD-BUSTERS

STOP AND THINK
COUNT TO 10
THINK HAPPY THOUGHTS
GET A DRINK OF WATER
TAKE DEEP BREATHS
READ A BOOK
TALK WITH AN ADULT
IGNORE THE SITUATION
EXERCISE
STAY CALM

WRITE OR DRAW ABOUT YOUR FEELINGS
LAUGH ABOUT IT
THINK OF CONSEQUENCES
LISTEN TO MUSIC
WATCH TV
PLAY A NON-VIOLENT VIDEOGAME
POUND A PILLOW
SQUISH CLAY
STROKE A PET
TAKE A NAP
USE SELF-TALK
WASH YOUR FACE IN COLD WATER
GO TO A COOLING-OFF PLACE

JOEY AND HIS BIG MESS

CLEAN UP CHOWDER

Appetizer Ingredients:

Master Chef:
- ☐ *Red Group Cards* (pages 152-160)
- ☐ *Blue Group Cards* (pages 161-162)
- ☐ Card stock
- ☐ Basket
- ☐ Chalkboard and chalk
- ☐ Timer

Student Chefs: (21 or more players—the game may be modified for fewer players)
- ☐ Large handles-affixed sports ball (optional—may be obtained from the physical education department)

Appetizer Preparation:

Reproduce the cards on cardstock. Cut the *Blue Group Cards* apart and place them in the basket. Decide how the *Red Group* members will reach the *Blue Group* members. They may close their eyes and try to find their way, leave their eyes open and hop to the right spot, or (and this is really fun) sit on a large sports ball with affixed handles and bounce to the right place.

Appetizer Activity:

Select nine students to be in the *Red Group.* Assign the rest of the students to the *Blue Group.*

Give each member of the *Red Group* a card. Then say:

> Find a place in the room far away from another *Red Group* member. Hold your card in front of you so others can see what you are.

> The rest of you are *Blue Group* members. You will form a line. When it is your turn to play, I will pull a card from the basket and read it aloud. The player must tell us where the item I have read belongs, then close his or her eyes and, as quickly as possible, find his or her way to that place. *(Players may also leave their eyes open and hop to that place or bounce to it on the sports ball.)* For example, if I would pull the card that says "books," the chosen student would say, "Books belong in a backpack." Then the chosen person must find his or her way to the person holding the backpack card. I will time the person trying to reach his or her partner and record it on the chalkboard. If, for some reason, the chosen person does not reach his or her partner, a zero is recorded. The pair with the fastest time will be the winners.

Begin the game.

(**Note:** For some Blue Group items there is more than one Red Group choice.)

TERRIFIC TIDY-UP TACOS

Main Course Ingredients:

Master Chef:
- [ ] *Joey And His Big Mess story* (pages 148-150)

Student Chefs:
- ✕ No materials required

Main Course Preparation:

None required.

Main Course Activity:

Read the following story aloud. Pause at the involvement questions for the children's answers.

Joey And His Big Mess

Joey was a kind little boy who made a big, ugly mess wherever he went. His biggest mess was in his bedroom.

"Joey," said his mother, "clean up your big mess."

Joey tried to clean his room. But it was such a big mess, he couldn't remember where to put everything. There were dirty clothes, clean clothes, shoes, socks, toys, soda cans, and two-week-old sandwiches! Joey didn't know what to do, so he picked his big mess up and took it with him.

As Joey and his mess were going down the stairs, he saw his brother.

"Joey," said his brother, pointing to the mess Joey had made in *his* room, "clean up your big mess."

Joey tried to clean his brother's room. But it was such a big mess, he couldn't remember where to put everything. There were candy wrappers, hats, books, skates, cards, tennis shoes, and dirty towels. Joey didn't know what to do. So he picked his big mess up from his brother's room and took it with him. Then he walked outside.

STOP Ask the children: "What is Joey's biggest problem?"

When Joey got outside, he saw his dad.

"Joey," said Dad pointing to the yard, "clean up your big mess."

Joey tried to clean up the yard. But it was such a big mess, he couldn't remember where to put everything. There were footballs, baseballs, beach balls, hockey sticks, tools, boxing gloves, skateboards, and a bicycle. Joey did not know what to do. So he picked up the big mess from the yard and took it with him.

Joey's mess was growing bigger and bigger! As a matter of fact, his mess had grown so big, it was hard to see Joey.

After school, Joey stopped by to see his grandmother. Grandmother loved Joey, but she did not love the big mess he was carrying with him. She didn't want him in the house with his big mess, so she gave him some milk and cookies on the front lawn.

Joey left his grandmother's with his big mess. Then he stopped to see his friends.

"Joey," said his friends, not wanting him in their clubhouse, "clean up your big mess."

STOP Ask the children: "What do you think will happen next?"

Everywhere Joey went, he was told to clean up his big mess. But instead of cleaning it up, he picked it up and took it with him.

Joey's mess grew bigger and BIGGER and **BIGGER!** It got so big, in fact, that it swallowed Joey!

STOP Ask the children: "How did Joey's mess get so big?"

Joey's mess got so big that his mother could not find him. His father could not find him. His brother could not find him. His grandmother could not find him, and his friends could not find him.

"We have to find Joey," they all said.

"I have an idea," said his brother. "Let's look for his trail."

"His trail?" asked his father.

"Yes," said his mother. "Joey leaves a messy trail wherever he goes. Let's look for the trail. That will help us find Joey."

"I see a trail of candy wrappers and empty cans," said his dad. "That will help us find Joey."

"Look!" said his mother. "I see a trail of dirty socks and tennis shoes. That will help us find Joey."

"I see a trail of puzzles and game pieces," said his brother. "That will help us find Joey."

"And I see a trail of spilled milk and cookie crumbs," said Grandmother. "That will help us find Joey."

STOP Ask the children to name some other clues that Joey left behind.

"Poor Joey!" they all cried.

Joey's messy trail took his family all over town. Soon everyone in town was looking for Joey.

Joey's trail led the long line of helpers to the park, where it stopped right near the beautiful fountain. Right in front of the fountain was the biggest pile of mess anyone had ever seen!

"Stand back!" the park guards yelled frantically when they saw the long line of helpers moving toward the big pile. "We have never seen anything like this. It must be destroyed!"

"But where is my Joey?" cried Joey's mother. "His trail stops here."

Then she heard a small voice. "I am here, Mother," said the voice.

"Joey, is that you?" they all asked.

"Yes, it's me. My big mess swallowed me up and I can't get out."

Everyone tried to help Joey. They decided the best way to get rid of Joey's big mess was to break it into small piles. So they all got big boxes with big labels and went to work on Joey's big mess.

There were boxes for shirts, slacks, socks, game pieces, puzzles, homework, dirty towels, and tennis shoes. There were boxes for candy wrappers, soda cans, cookie crumbs, and two-week-old sandwiches. There was even a special place for Joey's bicycle and for everything else in his big, messy pile.

Everyone worked hard sorting and putting things where they needed to be. After hours of working on Joey's big mess, they finally found Joey.

Joey stretched, then hugged his mom. "Whew! It's good to be free!" he exclaimed, brushing cookie crumbs from his hair.

STOP Ask the children: "Do you think Joey liked being trapped by his big mess?"

"What did you do with my big mess?" Joey asked.

"Come, let us show you," his dad replied.

When Joey saw his big mess, he was amazed. He learned that in his big mess were many things that he wanted and things that he needed but could never find.

"My skateboard," he said. "My jacket. My hat. My homework!"

That day, Joey decided he would never again be swallowed up by his big mess. He learned that each of his things should have a special place to go. In other words, everything should have its own special home.

STOP Ask the children: "Do you know where your things should go?"

Joey learned that his shoes' home was his closet, that the trash can was the home of empty cans and candy and gum wrappers, that his clean shirts had a home in his drawer, and that his dirty shirts had a different home.

Joey learned that everything he owned had a home. He learned that keeping everything in its own home kept his big mess away.

Joey's big mess tries to creep back every now and then, but Joey won't allow it.

And neither will his family.

FINISH the story by asking the children: "How will Joey keep his big mess away?"

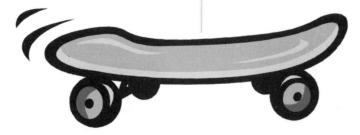

ORGANIZED BOX CAKE

Dessert Ingredients:

Master Chef:
- ☐ Newspaper
- ☐ Several colors of paint
- ☐ Several paint brushes
- ☐ Glitter, stickers, markers, and any other craft materials you wish
- ☐ Glue
- ☐ 2 Tables

Student Chefs:
- ☐ Small box with a lid

Dessert Preparation:

Cover a table with newspaper. Set out paint and paint brushes for the children to use. On another table, set out the glue and craft materials.

Dessert Activity:

Distribute a small box with a lid to each child. Then say:

Today, you are going to create a "home" for all of your pencils and other school supplies. Then you will not have to worry about having a big mess like Joey. Begin by coming to the paint table and painting your box. When it is dry, you may decorate it with any of the materials from the craft table. When you have finished decorating your box, put your things in it and keep it in your desk.

CLOSET

DRAWER

TRASH CAN

TOY CHEST

GUIDANCE FOR THE GOURMET RED GROUP CARDS © 2006 MAR*CO PRODUCTS, INC. 1-800-448-2197

GUIDANCE FOR THE GOURMET © 2006 MAR*CO PRODUCTS, INC. 1-800-448-2197

HAMPER

GUIDANCE FOR THE GOURMET RED GROUP CARDS © 2006 MAR*CO PRODUCTS, INC. 1-800-448-2197

BACKPACK

GYM BAG

WALLET

SHOES

CLEAN SHIRTS

DIRTY SOCKS

OLD FOOD

BASEBALL

HATS

SCHOOL BOOKS

PUZZLES

GAMES

EMPTY SODA CAN

MONEY

GYM CLOTHES

HOMEWORK

BASKETBALL

ENGLISH NOTEBOOK

WALLET-SIZE PICTURE OF A FRIEND

CANDY WRAPPER

DIRTY PAPER TOWELS

TROPHIES

SWIM GOGGLES

HUDSON HAROLDSON'S HAIR

APPETIZER

CLEAN-SWEEP APPLE BUTTER

Appetizer Ingredients:

Master Chef:
- ☐ Dustpan
- ☐ 2 brooms
- ☐ 2 apples

Student Chefs: (10 or more players)
- ✗ No materials required

Appetizer Preparation:

None required.

Appetizer Activity:

Divide the students into two teams and have the teams line up. Place the dustpan about 10 feet from the first person in line. Give the first person on each team a broom and an apple. Then say:

Place your apple on the floor. When I say "Go," the first player on each team must sweep the apple across the floor, around the dustpan, and back to the next person in line. Then the next person will do the same thing. This continues until every player has had a turn. The team who finishes first wins the game. This may sound easy, but apples are wobbly and can be hard to control. That is what makes this game so much fun!

Begin the game.

SPOTLESS SPINACH SOUP

Main Course Ingredients:

Master Chef:
- ☐ *Hudson Haroldson's Hair* story (pages 164-165)

Student Chefs:
- ✗ No materials required

Main Course Preparation:

None required.

Main Course Activity:

Read the following story aloud. Pause at the involvement questions for the children's answers.

Hudson Haroldson's Hair

"Oh my gosh!"
cried Hanna and Bess.
"Have you ever," said Jen,
"seen such a mess?"

There were bottles, rocks,
and oodles of string,
tadpoles and lizards,
and some slimy thing.

Pickles, pudding,
and a fat purple cow,
fish soup and spinach,
and we wonder, how?

"All of this crud,"
asked Campbell Sinclair,
"was found in
Hudson Haroldson's hair?"

STOP Ask the children: "What is Hudson's problem?"

"Hudson Haroldson!"
said Crystal Gleam.
"Don't you know
you must keep yourself clean!

"Wash that stuff out.
You know what to do.
Here's shampoo, water,
and a towel for you.

"Now wet and lather,
Scrub gently, then rinse.
When you get done,
you'll feel like a prince."

Well, Hudson did as she said,
and his hair looked great.
"Now isn't that better?"
asked Timothy Tate.

STOP Ask the children: "What did Crystal want Hudson to do?"

But the very next week
came the worst of their fears:
The crud was spotted
in Hudson's ears.

"Oh my gosh!"
cried Hanna and Bess.
"Have you ever," said Jen,
"seen such a mess?"

There were bottles, rocks,
and oodles of string,
tadpoles and lizards,
and some slimy thing.

Pickles, pudding,
and a fat purple cow,

fish soup and spinach,
and we wonder how …

It left his hair
and found his ears.
Believe it or not,
this happens, my dears.

"Hudson Haroldson!"
said Crystal Gleam.
"Don't you know
you must keep yourself clean?

"Wash that stuff out.
You know what to do.
Here is soap, a cloth,
and warm water for you."

STOP Ask the children: "What did Hudson use to clean his ears?"

"But it came back again,"
whispered Taylor and Keith.
"It left his ears
and found his teeth."

There were bottles, rocks,
and oodles of string,
tadpoles and lizards,
and some slimy thing.

Pickles, pudding,
and a fat purple cow,
fish soup and spinach,
and we wonder how …

It left his ears
and found his teeth
twice before
the end of the week.

"Hudson Haroldson!"
said Crystal Gleam.
"Don't you know
you must keep your teeth clean?

"Get that stuff off.
You know what to do.
Here's toothpaste, floss,
and a toothbrush for you."

Still, it happened once more:
A whole lot of mud
clung to his body,
along with the crud!

Hudson knew that
he'd better get clean
or he would hear from
Miss Crystal Gleam.

So he washed that stuff off.
He knew what to do.
He used soap and warm water
to take off the goo.

STOP Ask the children: "How did he get the crud off of his body?"

When he washed up this time,
his crud stayed away
'cause he cleaned himself up
each and every day!

He showered and flossed,
no slime in his ears.
He was squeaky clean
for the first time in years.

No more dirty trails
did he leave anywhere
from the crud in his ears,
teeth, and hair.

This clean-smelling prince
found a new friend today
named Allison Margarita
Millicent May.

FINISH the story by asking the children to name some things they should do each day to keep their bodies clean.

HYGIENE BASKET TURNOVERS

Dessert Ingredients:

Master Chef:
- ☐ Decorative tissue paper

Student Chefs:
- ☐ Hygiene products brought from home (Examples: soap, deodorant, tooth-paste, toothbrush, comb, brush, shampoo, small washcloth)
- ☐ Small basket or gift bag

Dessert Preparation:

Ask each child to bring a couple of hygiene products from home. Suggest items from the list above or assign certain items to each child. (**Note:** Many stores will donate products for this cause. The school nurse may also have hygiene goodies.)

Obtain a small basket or gift bag for each child.

Dessert Activity:

Give each child a small basket or gift bag and some tissue paper. Then say:

I want you to fill your baskets with this tissue paper and the personal hygiene items you have brought. When you have done this, I will ask you to display your items and tell how and why each one is used. When everyone has done this, you will exchange bags with another person.

SECTION 2
COPING SKILLS

WHEN LIFE SERVES UP BITTER GREENS

The purpose of this section is to help children cope with such tough issues as death, adult depression, and unsafe living environments.

PUT THE GREENS IN THE BOWL
(FACING THE ISSUE)

ADD FRUITS AND SPICES
(UNDERSTANDING EMOTIONS)

REMOVE THE TOUGH STEMS
(INFORMATION AND FACTS)

DRIZZLE WITH DRESSING
(COPING STRATEGIES)

TOSS AND EAT
(THERAPEUTIC ACTIVITIES)

WILTED NO-WEEP WATERCRESS TOSS: DEPRESSION IN FAMILIES
John-Michael's Eyes (Ages 6-10) .... page 169

SORROWFUL SORREL SALAD: GRIEF AND LOSS
Abby's Lullaby (Ages 6-12) .... page 179
After Grandpa Went Away (Ages 5-10) .... page 193

ANXIOUS ARUGULA SALAD: UNSAFE LIVING CONDITIONS
Yohawni's Backyard (Ages 6-12) .... page 200

JOHN-MICHAEL'S EYES
(Ages 6-10)

RECIPE: STEP 1

WILTED NO-WEEP WATERCRESS TOSS

PUT THE GREENS IN THE BOWL
(Facing The Issue)

Ingredients:

Master Chef:
- [ ] *John-Michael's Eyes* story (pages 169-171)

Student Chefs:
- [ ] Drawing paper
- [ ] Crayons

Preparation:

None required.

Activity:

Distribute drawing paper and crayons to the children. Read the following story aloud. Pause at the involvement questions for the children's answers.

John-Michael's Eyes

John-Michael's family lives in a peaceful home just west of Willow Creek, where friendly deer and playful squirrels often meet to drink and romp in the warm noonday sun.

John-Michael is a happy boy who is spirited and full of life. His mom says she can see the sunshine in his eyes.

His mom was always happy!
His mom was always busy!
She worked.
She cleaned.
She made things.
She baked.

STOP Ask the children: "What does your mom like to do?"

And she always gave hugs and kisses!

John-Michael loved his mom. In fact, she was the cause of the sunshine in his eyes.

Each day after school, John-Michael's mom met him at the bus stop with a gentle hug and a friendly smile.

Mom's hugs and smiles always made John-Michael feel safe and loved.

But today at the bus stop, there was no gentle hug. There was no friendly smile. Mom wasn't there.

"Mom must be lost," John-Michael thought, and he went home to look for her. He found her lying very still in her big, soft, white bed.

STOP Ask the children: "Where was his mom? Why was she in bed?"

At first, John-Michael seemed confused. Then his mom spoke. Her tender words always made him feel better. "I hope I didn't frighten you," she said slowly and faintly, as she softly stroked his cheek. "I must have fallen asleep. I feel tired today and a little mixed up."

"Mom does seem a little different," John-Michael thought, but he was glad that she wasn't too tired to give hugs and kisses.

With each passing day, Mom seemed more and more different. She began to look very tired and she was always mixed up. All day long, she did nothing but lay quietly in her big, soft white bed.

Soon she stopped singing. She stopped dancing. And she stopped doing all the fun things that had once made her smile.

Mom was not happy.
She was not busy.
She did not work.
She did not clean.
She did not make things.
She did not bake.
She did not smile.

STOP Ask the children: "How is John-Michael's mom feeling?"

But she still gave hugs and kisses!

John-Michael wanted his mother to be the person she used to be. He decided that cleaning his room—yuck!—and eating green vegetables—double yuck!—was the cure that would make his mom happy again.

So he carefully put away his red locomotive, his toy soldiers, and his remote-controlled car. He put away Spiky his big, ferocious dinosaur.

At dinner, he slurped down his mushy spinach and gobbled up his squishy, green peas. And he did it all for his mom.

But cleaning his room and eating spinach and green peas wasn't enough to cure his mother.

John-Michael felt frightened and all alone. He slowly and quietly left the dinner table to sit outside near the peaceful creek. The sunshine left his big, brown eyes and gave way to a flood of cold, bitter tears.

STOP Ask the children: "How is John-Michael feeling?"

As time passed, his mother stopped eating her spinach, her green peas, and everything else.

Dad tried to feed her, but she wouldn't eat. She cried a lot, she couldn't sleep.

Joey, my brother, sat on Dad's left knee. I sat on his right, and we all talked about Mom. Dad told us Mom needed the help of a special doctor called a *psychiatrist*. He said this special doctor often helps people who won't eat, can't sleep, and have stopped singing and dancing and doing all the fun things that once made them smile.

After Mom's examination, the special doctor told Dad she had a sickness called *depression*. He said she would need to spend time in a downtown hospital with other people who often felt the way she now feels.

STOP Ask the children: "What did the doctor say was wrong with Mom?"

The doctor also said Mom would be given little oval yellow pills called *anti-depressants*. The pills could help her feel better.

The kind, gentle doctor explained to my brother and me that Mom's sickness would not give her a runny nose or a fever like Joey's cold gave him last week. Mom's illness makes her feel sad, tired, scared, lonely, and very confused.

STOP Ask the children: "How is Mom feeling?"

My mom was not happy.
She was not busy.
She could not work.
She could not clean.
She could not make things.
She could not bake.
My mom COULD NOT give hugs and kisses!

In the cold, stillness of the car on the way home, we each silently cried. Our hearts hurt for Mom.

STOP Say: "John-Michael's whole family is sad. Use your drawing paper and crayons to draw a picture of John-Michael's family."

Dad took us to visit Mom at the downtown hospital each night after he made us dinner. It was very cold outside, so Dad bundled us up all snuggly and warm.

My dad always makes us feel safe and loved.

We visited with Mom in a large, friendly room where other patients were visiting with family members. Tonight Mom was sitting in a white wicker rocking chair near the thick glass window that overlooked the garden. She smiled when she saw us.

We gave her lots of hugs and kisses!

After many visits, we noticed that Mom was not tired and she wasn't all mixed-up like she had been. And last night, we all had dinner together in the hospital cafeteria!

Mom ate all of her food. She even ate her mushy spinach and her squishy, green peas.

The special doctor explained that our nightly visits, the oval yellow pills, and talking with someone called a *therapist* were all helping Mom feel better again.

STOP Ask the children: "What is helping John-Michael's mother feel better?"

The doctor said Mom was taking classes to learn more about her feelings and the feelings she had when she was a little girl. She even learned that long ago Grandma once had the same sad feelings that she now has. So did Grandma's mom, but that was a family secret.

Mom once told me feelings that hurt should never be kept secret.

STOP Ask the children: "Should anyone keep hurt feelings a secret?"

Soon after that, Mom left the downtown hospital with the friendly room and the garden and she came home to us. Once again …

She was happy!
She was busy!
She worked!
She cleaned!
She made things!
She baked!
She smiled!
And she gave LOTS of hugs and kisses!

Mom had brought back the sunshine. It beamed brightly in John-Michael's big brown eyes!

FINISH the story by asking the children: "How do you think John-Michael's family is feeling right now?"

ADD FRUITS AND SPICES
(Understanding Emotions)

Ingredients:

Master Chef:
- ✗ No materials required

Student Chefs:
- ☐ Copy of *How Are You Feeling Today?* (page 176)
- ☐ Pencil

Preparation:

Make a copy of *How Are You Feeling Today?* for each child.

Activity:

Distribute *How Are You Feeling Today?* and a pencil to each child. Then say:

> Everyone has feelings. And feelings are important. Without feelings, we would not know what makes us happy, sad, excited, mad, lonely, or jealous. It is important to know how you feel each and every day. Look at the list of feelings on your activity sheet. Think about how you feel today, right now. Then circle as many feelings as you need to.

When the children have finished, discuss the feelings they circled.

REMOVE THE TOUGH STEMS
(Information And Facts)

Ingredients:

Master Chef:
✗ No materials required

Student Chefs:
☐ Copy of *What Is Depression?* (page 177)
☐ Pencil

Preparation:

Make a copy of *What Is Depression?* for each child.

Activity:

Distribute *What Is Depression?* and a pencil to each child. Then say:

Read the definition of *depression* on the activity sheet. Answer the question and write the names of anyone you believe to be depressed on the petals of the flower.

WHAT IS DEPRESSION?

Most of us have sad feelings. But these feelings come and go. When sad feelings won't go away, that is called *depression*. Do you know anyone who has depression? Write that person's name on the petals of the flowers.

Words that might help you:

Mom
Neighbor
Brother
Aunt
Teacher

Dad
Grandma
Sister
Grandpa
Cousin

Uncle
Friend

GUIDANCE FOR THE GOURMET © 2006 MAR•CO PRODUCTS, INC. 1-800-448-2197

177

DRIZZLE WITH DRESSING
(Coping Strategies)

Ingredients:

Master Chef:

✗ No materials required

Student Chefs:

☐ Copy of *Wordfind* (page 178)
☐ Pencil

Preparation:

Make a copy of *Wordfind* for each child.

Activity:

Distribute the *Wordfind* and a pencil to each child. Then say:

> Look at the word list. These are words you heard in the story and may need to know. Find these words and circle them in the *Wordfind*. When you are finished, we will discuss their meanings.

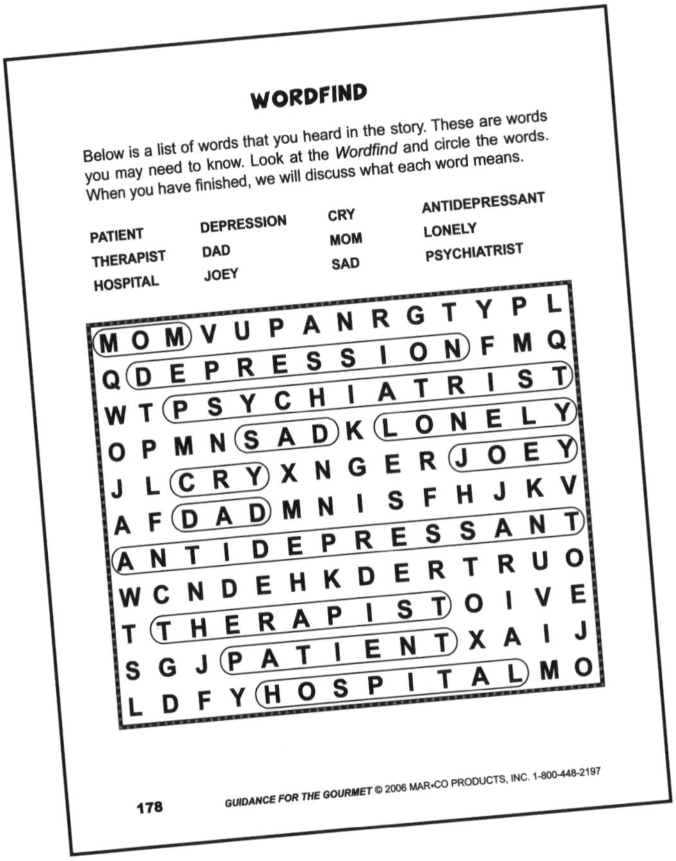

WORDFIND

Below is a list of words that you heard in the story. These are words you may need to know. Look at the *Wordfind* and circle the words. When you have finished, we will discuss what each word means.

PATIENT	DEPRESSION	CRY	ANTIDEPRESSANT
THERAPIST	DAD	MOM	LONELY
HOSPITAL	JOEY	SAD	PSYCHIATRIST

```
M O M V U P A N R G T Y P L
Q D E P R E S S I O N F M Q
W T P S Y C H I A T R I S T
O P M N S A D K L O N E L Y
J L C R Y X N G E R J O E Y
A F D A D M N I S F H J K V
A N T I D E P R E S S A N T
W C N D E H K D E R T R U O
T T H E R A P I S T O I V E
S G J P A T I E N T X A I J
L D F Y H O S P I T A L M O
```

178   GUIDANCE FOR THE GOURMET © 2006 MAR∗CO PRODUCTS, INC. 1-800-448-2197

TOSS AND EAT
(Therapeutic Activities)

Ingredients:

Master Chef:
- ☐ Sample *Get Well Bouquet*

Student Chefs:
- ☐ Large plastic cup
- ☐ Floral foam or clay
- ☐ Craft sticks
- ☐ Construction paper
- ☐ Colored tissue paper
- ☐ Ribbon
- ☐ Scissors
- ☐ Pencil or marker
- ☐ Glue

Preparation:

Following the activity directions, make a sample *Get Well Bouquet*.

Activity:

Begin the activity by saying:

You are going to create a beautiful floral arrangement for your loved one who is depressed. *(Display your completed* Get Well Bouquet.) Everything you need is on this table. Begin by drawing flowers and leaves on construction paper and cutting them out. You may write messages on the flowers such as, "I love you; I miss you; Get well; and other kind things you may wish to say. Then glue each flower and its leaves onto the craft sticks. Put the floral foam/clay into the bottom of the plastic cup. Stick the flowers in the floral foam. Cover the plastic cup with the tissue paper, then tie a ribbon around the cup.

HOW ARE YOU FEELING TODAY?

**Circle as many feelings as you need to.
Remember: Your feelings are important.**

SAD	MIXED UP	SCARED
NERVOUS	WORRIED	ANGRY
ALONE	SAFE	SICK
LOVED	HURT	BRAVE
GUILTY	EMBARRASSED	WEEPY
SILLY	I DON'T KNOW	HATEFUL

Write any feelings you have that were not listed above.

_____   _____

_____   _____

_____   _____

_____   _____

GUIDANCE FOR THE GOURMET © 2006 MAR∗CO PRODUCTS, INC. 1-800-448-2197

WHAT IS DEPRESSION?

Most of us have sad feelings. But these feelings come and go. When sad feelings won't go away, that is called *depression*. Do you know anyone who has depression? Write that person's name on the petals of the flowers.

Words that might help you:

Mom	Dad	
Neighbor	Grandma	
Brother	Sister	
Aunt	Grandpa	Uncle
Teacher	Cousin	Friend

WORDFIND

Below is a list of words that you heard in the story. These are words you may need to know. Look at the *Wordfind* and circle the words. When you have finished, we will discuss what each word means.

PATIENT	DEPRESSION	CRY	ANTIDEPRESSANT
THERAPIST	DAD	MOM	LONELY
HOSPITAL	JOEY	SAD	PSYCHIATRIST

```
M O M V U P A N R G T Y P L
Q D E P R E S S I O N F M Q
W T P S Y C H I A T R I S T
O P M N S A D K L O N E L Y
J L C R Y X N G E R J O E Y
A F D A D M N I S F H J K V
A N T I D E P R E S S A N T
W C N D E H K D E R T R U O
T T H E R A P I S T O I V E
S G J P A T I E N T X A I J
L D F Y H O S P I T A L M O
```

ABBY'S LULLABY
(Ages 6-12)

RECIPE: STEP 1

SORROWFUL SORREL SALAD

PUT THE GREENS IN THE BOWL
(Facing The Issue)

Ingredients:

Master Chef:
- ☐ *Abby's Lullaby* story (pages 179-185)

Student Chefs:
- ✗ No materials required

Preparation:

None required.

Activity:

Read the following story aloud. Pause at the involvement questions for the children's answers.

Abby's Lullaby

Abby and her grandma lived in a big yellow house near the old Chinaberry tree at the end of St. Francis Street. Abby's mom, dad, and her doll "Tootie" lived there, too.

Grandma and Abby did lots of fun things together. They played hide-and-seek, they baked homemade cookies, and they had elegant tea parties.

After a long hard rain, Grandma and Abby would sit in the backyard near the slippery mud puddles and make sticky mud cakes just like Grandma did when she was a little girl.

Each Friday morning, Grandma visited with her good friend, Mrs. Jenny. Grandma and Mrs. Jenny would sit on the big wooden porch, eat pancakes and fried apples, and sip black coffee while they talked about grown-up stuff.

STOP Ask the children: "Did Abby like being with her grandma?"

Each night at bedtime, Grandma would say, "Come along now, Abby. It's time for bed." Then she would tuck Abby in with her pink fuzzy ballerina blanket, kiss her on the forehead, and sing her this special bedtime song:

Close your eyes, it's time to sleep.
Tucked in safely, from arms to feet.
Lay down your weary head, my dear.
Love keeps you safe, no need to fear.
Think on those things that make you smile.
This darkness lasts but a little while.
The cloud of night will soon fade away.
Sweet light will proclaim a brand new day.
So close your eyes—no need to fear.
Love keeps you safe. Now, sleep, my dear.

Grandma's song always seemed to help Abby sleep peacefully and dream sweet dreams.

STOP Ask the children: "Why do you think the song made Abby feel safe?"

One quiet night after Grandma's soothing song, Abby looked up at her grandmother's gentle, round face and asked if she would give their bedtime song a name.

Grandma smiled while pretending to ponder, "Hmmm, let's see now," she said. "Why don't we call it *Abby's Lullaby*?"

"*Abby's Lullaby?* What's a lullaby, Grandma?" asked Abby.

"A *lullaby*, my dear," Grandma answered, as she stroked Abby's soft, fluffy hair, "is a special song to help little girls just like you feel peaceful and safe. Every child needs a lullaby, Abby." Grandma then kissed Abby's forehead and tucked her in.

The next morning, Abby awoke to the smell of Grandma's old-fashioned buttermilk pancakes. She grabbed Tootie and ran downstairs. She kissed Grandma good morning and took her place at the breakfast table to watch Grandma flip those scrumptious, mouth-watering pancakes that sizzled in the old black cast iron skillet.

Grandma had a talent for making her buttermilk pancakes perform perfect acrobatic aerials.

STOP Ask the children: "What are *acrobatic aerials*?"

But Grandma seemed different this morning.

"Grandma is moving slowly," noted Abby. "And she's not talking to Tootie and me."

Grandma carefully placed the golden brown pancakes on Abby's favorite plate, the one with the little pink- and white-slippers. When Grandma turned to serve Abby, she became wobbly and Abby's plate slipped from her hand and crashed to the floor. Almost falling, Grandma managed to steady herself by holding onto the back of Abby's chair.

"Grandma?" asked Abby. "Are you OK?"

"I'm fine," Grandma answered faintly. "I just need to sit and rest a bit." Somehow she gathered enough strength to make more pancakes, serve Abby, and clean the kitchen floor. Then she carefully made her way to her soft green chair. She sat there and napped all morning.

STOP Ask the children: "How is Grandma feeling?"

Abby took her pink fuzzy ballerina blanket and tucked it around Grandma.

Around lunchtime, Abby decided she and Tootie would make peanut butter sandwiches. They used the lace doilies and fancy china saucers like Grandma used when she and Abby had their elegant tea parties.

Abby tried to serve Grandma, but she wouldn't eat. She just sat in her soft green chair, wrapped in Abby's pink fuzzy ballerina blanket, and napped.

Suddenly, Abby didn't feel hungry any more.

When Mom and Dad arrived home from work, the friendly glow of the bright yellow porch light didn't welcome them as it had done each night before. A strange shadow seemed to loom over the brightly painted house at the end of St. Francis Street.

RECIPE: STEP 1

STOP Ask the children: "Why did things seem strange on Abby's street?"

When Mom and Dad entered the house, it didn't smell of the wonderfully delicious aroma of Grandma's home cooking. Grandma was still napping in her big soft green chair.

Abby knew Mom and Dad were worried when they gave her a strong hug and a gentle kiss and told her Mrs. Jenny was going to stay with her while they took Grandma to the hospital to visit with Dr. Stephens.

"Grandma must really not be feeling well," thought Abby.

When Mom and Dad returned from the hospital, Abby and Mrs. Jenny were sitting at the breakfast table reading Abby's favorite bedtime story, *Belinda, The Sleepy Ballerina.*

"Where is Grandma?" Abby asked anxiously as they entered the kitchen. Mom's eyes welled with tears as she calmly responded, "Abby, we need to talk."

Mrs. Jenny's eyes welled with tears, too, and she decided it was time for her to leave.

STOP Ask the children: "What do you think happened?"

Dad held Mom's hand tightly as they struggled to explain that while Grandma was at the hospital, her heart stopped beating and she stopped breathing.

"Grandma is not coming home ever again, Abby," Mom said. "She passed away. Grandma passed away, Abby."

Abby stood very still.

She had no feelings.

She had no words.

Slowly, she made her way to Grandma's big soft chair.

She stopped and stared.

Then, slowly and cautiously, she grabbed her pink fuzzy blanket from Grandma's soft green chair and ran upstairs.

Abby now understands the pain of a broken heart.

STOP Ask the children: "Have you ever felt like Abby?"

Mom and Dad hurried to comfort Abby. They wrapped their arms around her and held her close.

"It's not fair," she sobbed. "I need her, Dad. I didn't even say goodbye. Why did she leave me, Mom? Did I do something wrong?"

"No, no, Abby," Mom responded. "It was not your fault. Death happens to everything and everyone. It even happens to good people like Grandma."

There were no words that Mom or Dad could say to ease Abby's pain. Much later, she fell asleep in the safe and warm embrace of her parents' arms.

(***Note:*** The following portion of the story addresses traditional funerals/burials. If this is not appropriate for the children to whom the story is being presented, skip this portion and resume with the alternate ending where indicated on page 184.)

The next day, Abby's house was filled with visitors. Some brought food, some brought cards and flowers, and some brought nothing at all. But everyone was thinking of her grandmother.

Mom and Dad left to visit with Mr. Renquist about the next day's funeral service (memorial service) for Grandma. Mom explained that at the service, family members, neighbors, and friends all would come to say goodbye to Grandma.

Tonight, Grandma will have a *wake (viewing)*. Mom explained that Grandma will be lying in a beautiful white coffin. A coffin is a special bed-like box for people whose hearts have stopped beating.

STOP Ask the children: "Are there any words that we have talked about that you are not sure you understand?" Then discuss the different ways to say goodbye to a loved one and have the children share their remembrances of their loved ones' services.

Mom said, "Many people will attend Grandma's wake (viewing). Some will cry. Some will smile. Some will do nothing at all. But all of them will be thinking of Grandma."

The next morning, all of our family members met at our house for the funeral procession. My Uncle Buster was there. So was my Aunt Helen.

STOP Explain different ways people may arrive at the service. Have the children explain how they went to the service.

Most of my relatives were dressed in black. I wore the pleated yellow dress that Grandma made for me on my birthday. She liked my dress so well, she made herself one, too.

STOP Ask the children: "Why do you think Abby wore her yellow dress?"

Three limousines lined were up near our house, on the side of the street opposite the old Chinaberry tree. The long black cars were there to take us to say goodbye to Grandma.

"Grandma and I can't bake cookies any more," thought Abby.

When we arrived at the place where Grandma was waiting, we lined up near the big brown double doors with the shiny brass handles. As we entered the building, I saw my grandma. She looked as though she was lying in the middle of a beautiful colorful flower garden. She was wearing her pleated yellow dress. Just like mine.

STOP Tell the children that in some cases, the coffin is open and friends and relatives may view the body. In other cases, the coffin is closed. And in some cases, there is no coffin. Then have those children who wish to do so tell how this was handled at the service they attended.

"How pretty Grandma looks," thought Abby.

Many people lined up to look at Grandma. Some smiled. Some cried. Some did nothing at all. I walked up to see her face. She looked cold and still. I slipped her favorite picture of me into the palm of her right hand.

"I love you, Grandma," Abby whispered.

"Grandma and I can't have tea parties any more," thought Abby.

During the service, everybody said goodbye. Some sang. Some spoke. Some did nothing at all. But all of them were thinking of Grandma.

When the service was over, Grandma's coffin was placed in a hearse. Her beautiful colorful flower garden was placed there, too. I held on very tightly to Mom and Dad's hands.

"Grandma and I can't make mud cakes any more," thought Abby.

STOP Ask the children: "How do you think Abby is feeling?"

We drove to the cemetery, where we sat in rows on white wooden chairs underneath a huge green-and-gold tent Mom called a *canopy*.

Mom and Dad said that after this ceremony, Grandma's body would be laid to rest in a special spot here that Grandma chose long ago.

"Grandma and I can't play hide-and-seek any more," Abby thought.

Mr. Renquist gave Mom and Dad a cream-colored book beautifully decorated with thin, golden thread. In the book were the names of everyone who had come to say goodbye to Grandma. Mom and Dad gave the special book to Aunt Helen and Uncle Buster.

Mr. Renquist then gave everyone a pretty sheet of rose-colored paper. On the inside of that sheet was a story about Grandma's life. On the outside was her picture. Underneath her picture were two important dates: the date her life began and the date her life ended.

"Grandma is gone," thought Abby. "We can't bake cookies. We can't have tea parties. We can't make mud cakes. We can't play hide-and-seek … and we can't sing our special bedtime song."

Abby covered her face with her tiny, trembling hands and wept.

STOP Ask the children: "How would you make Abby feel better?"

After a short graveside service, Mr. Renquist thanked everyone for coming and asked if anyone had any last words.

"It is now time for Grandma to rest," thought Abby.

Then, slowly and courageously, Abby stood up. "I have one last thing to say," she announced.

"My grandma is gone and she can't sing to me any more, so I would now like to sing our special song for her. And so she began …

> Close your eyes, it's time to sleep.
> Tucked in safely, from arms to feet.
> Lay down your weary head, my dear.
> Love keeps you safe, no need to fear.
> Think on those things that make you smile.
> This darkness lasts but a little while.
> The cloud of night will soon fade away.
> Sweet light will proclaim a brand new day.
> So close your eyes—no need to fear.
> Love keeps you safe. Now, sleep, my dear.

Abby turned and looked out among to audience and said, "Every grandma needs a lullaby."

Everyone wept.

FINISH the story by asking the children: "Why did Abby sing her special song?"

Written in loving memory of Mrs. Ella B. Stephens and Mrs. Ismay Hope Cook.

(**Note:** If the portion of the story on traditional funerals was omitted, continue the story from this point.)

The next day many visitors came to Abby's home. Some brought flowers, some brought food, and some brought nothing at all. But all were thinking of Abby's Grandmother.

Mrs. Jenny brought over a dozen of Abby's favorite peanut butter cookies. The cookies were soft and warm and their rich, thick aroma filled the busy room. The smell of the cookies flooded Abby's mind with happy thoughts. Abby began to smile, but her smile faded away when she thought "Grandma and I can't bake cookies anymore."

Later that day, the sky darkened and fresh, plump rain drops burst from the heavy clouds. Abby stood by the window and watched as the pouring rain turned the rich soil into sticky mud. She imagined that she and Grandma were sitting in the mud playing as they had done many times before. Abby began to smile, but her smile faded away when she thought, "Grandma and I can't make mud cakes any more."

STOP Ask the children: "Why is Abby so sad?"

Abby thought of her Grandmother all day. She thought of the elegant tea parties and the soothing bedtime stories. "I miss my grandma," whimpered Abby breathlessly. "Why did she have to go?" Abby began to cry.

Abby was sad for a long time and for a while it seemed like she'd never be happy again. Most days she did nothing but lay in Grandma's soft green chair with Tootie and her pink ballerina blanket and slept.

After many days, Abby decided that she did not want to be sad anymore. "Grandma would not want me to be sad," she thought. "She would want me to be brave."

Abby's mom and dad knew that it would not be easy for Abby to be brave. Abby missed her grandmother terribly, so did her parents and all of her grandmother's friends.

Everyone knew that Abby would need their help.

Abby and her parents decided to make a special box and fill it with all of Grandma and Abby's favorite things. Abby and her mother found an old wooden box in the attic.

They cleaned the box and polished it as carefully as Abby's grandmother cleaned the dishes after she made those mouth-watering meals. They lined the inside of the box with soft, white stuffing and covered the stuffing with pieces of left over colorful cloth from one of the many dresses that Grandma had made for Abby. Then they polished the box with the lemon oil that Grandma used to make the dining room table all shiny and sweet.

When the box was done, Abby thought long and hard about the things she wanted to place in it.

STOP Ask the children: "What kinds of things do you think Abby will put in her special box?"

First, she put in leaves that she had gently pulled from the Chinaberry tree where she and Grandma played hide and seek together.

Then she added a tiny saucer wrapped in a lace doily that Grandma used at their elegant tea parties.

Then she put in all the cookie recipes that she and her grandmother used when they baked together.

That night Dad wrote down the words to the special lullaby that Grandma sang to Abby to place in her special box.

Dad knew the words, because Abby sang it even when it was not her bedtime. As Abby read the words to the lullaby that rested in her dad's ample hands, she remembered the love and warmth that she felt each time Grandma sang it to her. Then she carefully took the precious gift from her father and began to sing:

> Close your eyes, it's time to sleep.
> Tucked in safely, from arms to feet.
> Lay down your weary head, my dear.
> Love keeps you safe, no need to fear.
> Think on those things that make you smile.
> This darkness lasts but a little while.
> The cloud of night will soon fade away.
> Sweet light will proclaim a brand new day.
> So close your eyes—no need to fear.
> Love keeps you safe. Now, sleep, my dear.

After Abby sang her lullaby, she held it close to her heart. She then folded it ever so carefully and placed it on top of all of her other treasures.

Feeling content, she slowly closed her treasure box and then closed her sleepy eyes knowing that special memories of Grandma would always be in her heart and in her special box.

FINISH the story by asking the children: "Why do you think Abby placed the lullaby on top of all her other treasures?"

Written in loving memory of Mrs. Ella B. Stephens and Mrs. Ismay Hope Cook.

ADD FRUITS AND SPICES
(Understanding Emotions)

Ingredients:

Master Chef:
- ✗ No materials required

Student Chefs:
- ☐ Copy of *Feelings* (page 190)
- ☐ Pencil

Preparation:

Reproduce *Feelings* for each child.

Activity:

Distribute *Feelings* and a pencil to each child. Then say:

> When you lose someone you love, you may have many different feelings. Look at the activity sheet and think about the day you heard your loved one had passed away. Remember it clearly in your mind and review the feelings you had. Look at the feelings listed on your activity sheet and circle those that match how you felt. If you had other feelings, write them on the page.

When the children have finished, discuss the feelings they circled or wrote down.

FEELINGS

Think back to when you heard that your loved one had passed away. How did you feel? Circle the feelings you had and add any other feelings that you had at that time.

alone	numb	guilty
shocked	frightened	sad
angry	confused	upset

I just pretended it never happened

Write any other feelings you had.

_____   _____
_____   _____
_____   _____
_____   _____

REMOVE THE TOUGH STEMS
(Information And Facts)

Ingredients:

Master Chef:
✗ No materials required

Student Chefs:
☐ Copy of *Life And Death* (page 191)
☐ Pencil

Preparation:

Reproduce *Life And Death* for each child.

Activity:

Distribute *Life and Death* and a pencil to each child. Then say:

Read the first sentences on your activity page. Then we will discuss how each of the living things mentioned changed after death. *(Pause until the children have done this.)* Now read the next sentence.

Getting sick is something that happens to everyone. Read the three sentences about getting sick. *(Pause until the children have done this.)* Now I want you to finish the activity sheet by telling about your loved one who passed away. *(Pause until the children have done this.)*

Have the children share what they have written about their loved ones who passed away. Complete the activity sheet by having the children contribute answers for the *Point To Ponder* question.

LIFE AND DEATH

Life and death are all around us. How do these living things change after death?

a flower …
grass …
a fish …
a frog …
leaves …
a pet hamster …

All living things die: flowers, grass, fish, frogs, leaves, pet hamsters. Sometimes so do people we love and care for.

GETTING SICK

All of our bodies get sick at times. Being sick doesn't mean that you will die. But sometimes a body gets so sick that it can't get better again.

Tell me about your loved one who passed away.

Name _____

Relationship _____

What happened? _____

_____

Point to Ponder: How is sleep different from death?

191

GUIDANCE FOR THE GOURMET © 2006 MAR•CO PRODUCTS, INC. 1-800-448-2197

DRIZZLE WITH DRESSING
(Coping Strategies)

Ingredients:

Master Chef:

  ✗ No materials required

Student Chefs:

  ☐ Copy of *What To Do About My Feelings* (page 192)

Preparation:

Reproduce *What To Do About My Feelings* for each child.

Activity:

Distribute *What To Do About My Feelings* to each child. Then read the information with the children and discuss any topic as long as it is beneficial for the children.

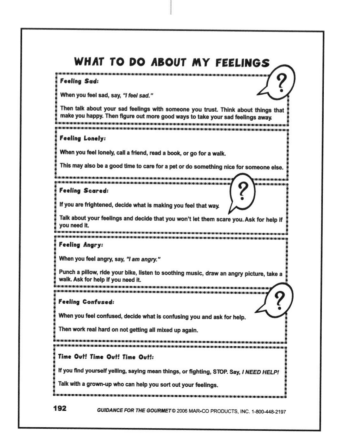

TOSS AND EAT
(Therapeutic Activities)

Ingredients:

Master Chef:
- ☐ Sample *Memory Box*
- ☐ Decorative items such as beads, glitter, buttons, yarn, and ribbons
- ☐ Table

Student Chefs:
- ☐ Shoe box or any box with a lid
- ☐ Picture of the loved one who passed away
- ☐ Items that remind the child of the loved one who passed away
- ☐ Glue
- ☐ Construction paper
- ☐ Colored tissue paper
- ☐ Scissors
- ☐ Pencil
- ☐ Crayons or markers

Preparation:

This activity works best in two sessions. In the first session, have the children decorate their boxes and prepare to bring in their pictures and memory items. After the children have decorated their boxes, let them dry until the next session. Then have the children complete their boxes with the items they have brought from home.

Make a sample *Memory Box* by following the activity directions. Put the decorative materials, boxes, and supplies on a table.

Activity:

Begin the activity by saying:

Today, you are going to create a *Memory Box* about your loved one who has passed away. *(Display your completed* Memory Box.) Everything you need is on this table. Begin by choosing whatever materials you would like to use to decorate the outside of your box. Then use them to decorate your box. When you have finished, set your box aside and let it dry. *(Do not continue this activity until the* Memory Boxes *are completely dry.)*

Select some tissue paper and use it to line the inside of the box. Be sure to not put so much tissue paper in your box that there is no room left for your remembrance articles. Next, glue the picture of your special person to the outside of your box. Then fill the box with things that remind you of that special person.

Take your box home and put it in a special place. Whenever you think about your special person, take your box out and look at the mementos you have saved.

Before taking their boxes home, have the children share what they have done.

FEELINGS

Think back to when you heard that your loved one had passed away. How did you feel? Circle the feelings you had and add any other feelings that you had at that time.

alone   numb   guilty

shocked   frightened   sad

angry   confused   upset

I just pretended it never happened.

Write any other feelings you had.

_____   _____

_____   _____

_____   _____

_____   _____

LIFE AND DEATH

Life and death are all around us. How do these living things change after death?

a flower …
grass …
a fish …
a frog …
leaves …
a pet hamster …

All living things die: flowers, grass, fish, frogs, leaves, pet hamsters. Sometimes so do people we love and care for.

GETTING SICK

All of our bodies get sick at times. Being sick doesn't mean that you will die. But sometimes a body gets so sick that it can't get better again.

Tell me about your loved one who passed away.

Name _____

Relationship _____

What happened? _____

_____

_____

Point to Ponder: How is sleep different from death?

WHAT TO DO ABOUT MY FEELINGS

Feeling Sad:

When you feel sad, say, *"I feel sad."*

Then talk about your sad feelings with someone you trust. Think about things that make you happy. Then figure out more good ways to take your sad feelings away.

Feeling Lonely:

When you feel lonely, call a friend, read a book, or go for a walk.

This may also be a good time to care for a pet or do something nice for someone else.

Feeling Scared:

If you are frightened, decide what is making you feel that way.

Talk about your feelings and decide that you won't let them scare you. Ask for help if you need it.

Feeling Angry:

When you feel angry, say, *"I am angry."*

Punch a pillow, ride your bike, listen to soothing music, draw an angry picture, take a walk. Ask for help if you need it.

Feeling Confused:

When you feel confused, decide what is confusing you and ask for help.

Then work real hard on not getting all mixed up again.

Time Out! Time Out! Time Out!:

If you find yourself yelling, saying mean things, or fighting, STOP. Say, *I NEED HELP!*

Talk with a grown-up who can help you sort out your feelings.

AFTER GRANDPA WENT AWAY
(Ages 5-10)

RECIPE: STEP 1

SORROWFUL SORREL SALAD

PUT THE GREENS IN THE BOWL
(Facing The Issue)

Ingredients:

Master Chef:
- ☐ *After Grandpa Went Away* (pages 193-194)

Student Chefs:
- ✗ No materials required

Preparation:

None required.

Activity:

Read the following story aloud. Pause at the involvement questions for the children's answers.

After Grandpa Went Away
(A young boy's ode to his grandfather)

After Grandpa went away,
I felt lonely and sad.
So did my mother,
my grandma, and Dad.

I don't understand
why he had to go.
I need him with me.
How I miss him so.

He taught me to hunt
and to swim at age three.
There was no Grandpa
better than he.

He taught me to hike
and to catch my first fish.
To have him back,
is my only wish.

I know it won't happen.
I know it can't be.
But I still wish Grandpa
were right here with me.

STOP Ask the children: "What happened to the boy's grandfather?"

His heart is what did it.
It didn't work right.
It made him real sick,
and stopped beating one night.

They tried to save him,
but it was his time to go.
I love you Grandpa
and I miss you so.

I remember the things
that you said to me
about life and stuff
while I sat on your knee.

Sometimes I feel hurt
and don't know what to do,
so I get mad and blame others
for not having you.

But it's no one's fault,
and that I do know.
It's just hard, Grandpa,
to let you go.

I'll miss you so much
each and every season.
I've written below
a few of the reasons.

Like knowing this fall
my first game you won't see!
But I'll run and I'll score,
just like you taught me.

This winter I'll miss
the snow fights we had,
and how you and I hammered
Mom and Dad!

I'll miss the fine garden
that we planted each spring,
and that silly song
you taught me to sing.

STOP Ask the children: "What are some things that the boy and his Grandpa did together?"

I'll miss summers most,
and all the fun in the park,
where we swam and went boating
'till way after dark.

But I'll take time to remember,
if just for a while
the fun stuff we did
that still makes me smile.

I'll remember the trouble
that we both got into
for playing games one school night
'til a quarter past two.

The time we played catch
in the rain me and you,
and had to change our clothes
that were soaked through and through.

Yes, you are gone,
and when I feel sad,
I'll cling to those memories
of the fun we both had.

I'll let them cheer me
when I start to feel blue,
and be happy I once had
a grandpa like you.

FINISH the story by asking the children: "How do you remember your loved one?"

Written in loving memory of Willie F. Stephens.

(**Note:** The activities that follow the story *After Grandpa Went Away* are identical to the ones for *Abby's Lullaby*.)

ADD FRUITS AND SPICES
(Understanding Emotions)

Ingredients:

Master Chef:
- ✗ No materials required

Student Chefs:
- ☐ Copy of *Feelings* (page 190)
- ☐ Pencil

Preparation:

Reproduce *Feelings* for each child.

Activity:

Distribute *Feelings* and a pencil to each child. Then say:

> When you lose someone you love, you may have many different feelings. Look at the activity sheet and think about the day you heard your loved one had passed away. Remember it clearly in your mind and review the feelings you had. Look at the feelings listed on your activity sheet and circle those that match how you felt. If you had other feelings, write them on the page.

When the children have finished, discuss the feelings they circled or wrote down.

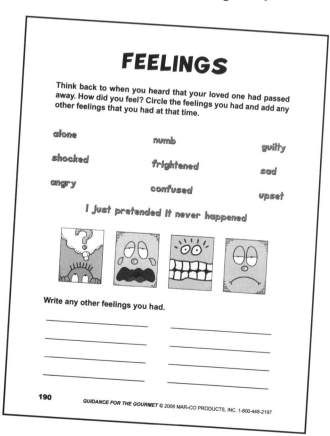

FEELINGS

Think back to when you heard that your loved one had passed away. How did you feel? Circle the feelings you had and add any other feelings that you had at that time.

alone   numb   guilty

shocked   frightened   sad

angry   confused   upset

I just pretended it never happened

Write any other feelings you had.

_____   _____

_____   _____

_____   _____

_____   _____

190 GUIDANCE FOR THE GOURMET © 2006 MAR•CO PRODUCTS, INC. 1-800-448-2197

REMOVE THE TOUGH STEMS
(Information And Facts)

Ingredients:

Master Chef:

✗ No materials required

Student Chefs:

☐ Copy of *Life And Death* (page 191)
☐ Pencil

Preparation:

Reproduce *Life And Death* for each child.

Activity:

Distribute *Life and Death* and a pencil to each child. Then say:

> Read the first sentences on your activity page. Then we will discuss how each of the living things mentioned changed after death. *(Pause until the children have done this.)* Now read the next sentence.

> Getting sick is something that happens to everyone. Read the three sentences about getting sick. *(Pause until the children have done this.)* Now I want you to finish the activity sheet by telling about your loved one who passed away. *(Pause until the children have done this.)*

Have the children share what they have written about their loved ones who passed away. Complete the activity sheet by having the children contribute answers for the *Point To Ponder* question.

LIFE AND DEATH

Life and death are all around us. How do these living things change after death?

a flower …
grass …
a fish …
a frog …
leaves …
a pet hamster …

All living things die: flowers, grass, fish, frogs, leaves, pet hamsters. Sometimes so do people we love and care for.

GETTING SICK

All of our bodies get sick at times. Being sick doesn't mean that you will die. But sometimes a body gets so sick that it can't get better again.

Tell me about your loved one who passed away.

Name _____

Relationship _____

What happened? _____
_____
_____

Point to Ponder: How is sleep different from death?

191

DRIZZLE WITH DRESSING
(Coping Strategies)

Ingredients:

Master Chef:
✗ No materials required

Student Chefs:
☐ Copy of *What To Do About My Feelings* (page 192)

Preparation:

Reproduce *What To Do About My Feelings* for each child.

Activity:

Distribute *What To Do About My Feelings* to each child. Then read the information with the children and discuss any topic as long as it is beneficial for the children.

TOSS AND EAT
(Therapeutic Activities)

Ingredients:

Master Chef:
- ☐ Sample *Memory Box*
- ☐ Decorative items such as beads, glitter, buttons, yarn, and ribbons
- ☐ Table

Student Chefs:
- ☐ Shoe box or any box with a lid
- ☐ Picture of the loved one who passed away
- ☐ Items that remind the child of the loved one who passed away
- ☐ Glue
- ☐ Construction paper
- ☐ Colored tissue paper
- ☐ Scissors
- ☐ Pencil
- ☐ Crayons or markers

Preparation:

This activity works best in two sessions. In the first session, have the children decorate their boxes and prepare to bring in their pictures and memory items. After the children have decorated their boxes, let them dry until the next session. Then have the children complete their boxes with the items they have brought from home.

Make a sample *Memory Box* by following the activity directions. Put the decorative materials, boxes, and supplies on a table.

Activity:

Begin the activity by saying:

Today, you are going to create a *Memory Box* about your loved one who has passed away. *(Display your completed* Memory Box.) Everything you need is on this table. Begin by choosing whatever materials you would like to use to decorate the outside of your box. Then use them to decorate your box. When you have finished, set your box aside and let it dry. *(Do not continue this activity until the* Memory Boxes *are completely dry.)*

Select some tissue paper and use it to line the inside of the box. Be sure to not put so much tissue paper in your box that there is no room left for your remembrance articles. Next, glue the picture of your special person to the outside of your box. Then fill the box with things that remind you of that special person.

Take your box home and put it in a special place. Whenever you think about your special person, take your box out and look at the mementos you have saved.

Before taking their boxes home, have the children share what they have done.

★★★★★ EXTRA!!

SPECIAL CONDIMENTS FOR SORROWFUL SORREL

GUIDELINES FOR HELPING CHILDREN COPE WITH DEATH AND DYING

Provide young children with clear and honest age-appropriate facts about the death of a loved one.

Ask about the child's concept of death. Be aware that some young children may have a difficult time distinguishing reality from fantasy.

Pay attention to the child's emotional state. Be available to answer questions and to nurture as the child experiences grief emotions.

Do not associate *death* with *sleep*. Emphasize that death is permanent. Confusing death with sleep may make some children anxious about falling asleep.

Do not avoid the topic of death when the child wants to discuss it. Be prepared to patiently answer the same questions over and over about the death of a loved one.

Be vigilant. Some young children may not be able to verbally express what they are feeling and may, instead, act out. Be available to redirect, comfort, and encourage the child to express emotions in a less-hostile manner.

Expect crying, anger, confusion, depression, sleep interruptions, loss of appetite, and concerns about losing other loved ones.

Inform the child's school, classmates, close friends, and adult leader's of groups in which he/she participates of the child's loss.

Seek the help of friends, family members, counselors, religious leaders, and support groups, if necessary.

YOHAWNI'S BACKYARD
(Ages 6-12)

RECIPE: STEP 1

ANXIOUS ARUGULA SALAD

PUT THE GREENS IN THE BOWL
(Facing The Issue)

Ingredients:

Master Chef:
- [ ] *Yohawni's Backyard* (pages 200-202)

Student Chefs:
- [ ] Drawing paper
- [ ] Crayons

Preparation:

None required.

Activity:

Distribute drawing paper and crayons to the children. Then read the following story aloud. Pause at the involvement questions for the children's answers.

Yohawni's Backyard

Yohawni's balcony has always been her secret place to dream. One night, she closed her eyes and dreamed a soft white cloud came down from the sky and took her away from her tiny apartment, the screaming sirens, the thundering music, and the many rude voices.

The cloud took her to a special place … a peaceful place … where the grass was green and the air was sweet; a place where Yohawni had a home … a beautiful home … with her very own backyard.

STOP Ask the children: "Did you ever dream of a special place? What is it like?"

In Yohawni's dream, her beautiful home was a palace. She was the great Queen Yohawni who sat proudly upon her throne.

Her magnificent castle had rooms that were large and bright. Yohawni gave the best room to her mother. In her mother's room, there was a fine-looking bed with sweet-smelling sheets, just like the beds in the home where Yohawni's mother scrubbed floors each day.

Yohawni gave her mother royal servants who gladly washed her thick braided hair and rubbed warm oils onto her aching shoulders, hands, and feet. They even painted yellow butterflies on the nails of her mother's ebony toes.

Yohawni then gave her mother a grand hat and a fancy polka dot dress just like the one her mother ironed for Mrs. Hightower. Yohawni's mother looked like a queen, so Yohawni gladly gave her mother her own beautiful palace and her own royal throne.

STOP Ask the children: "What is Yohawni's mother's job?"

Yohawni blinked, and her backyard became a garden full of brightly-colored flowers, friendly animals, and trees with delicious fruit. The trees fed the animals. The animals sang to the trees. The flowers made the animals brave and made everything pretty. When Yohawni walked in her garden, she smiled because her garden made her happy.

Other children heard of Yohawni's happy garden and came to visit when their moms had to work. The trees fed the children, the animals sang to them, and the pretty flowers made them feel strong and brave.

The children laughed and danced in Yohawni's garden. Yohawni knew the children's faces. She knew their voices. Yohawni was pleased that they were in her garden and that her garden made them happy.

Then the rain came. Yohawni's backyard quickly became a beach with soft wet sand and deep blue water. The soft wet sand touched the deep blue water while the bright yellow sun warmed the sand and the water.

People were standing in the warm sand, waiting to be touched by the soothing blue water. It made Yohawni happy to see them there.

From the soft wet sand Yohawni heard her mother's gentle voice. "Yohawni," she said, "wake up." It was time to return, so her imaginary white cloud lifted her from the beach and took her back to the balcony of her second-floor apartment.

Yohawni told her mother all about her dream. As her mother listened, she smiled as brightly as the yellow sun that warmed the soft wet sand on Yohawni's imaginary beach. "Yohawni," said her mother, "last night I had a dream that a star came down from the sky and took me back to a place that my great grandfather owned many, many years ago. It was a special place … a peaceful place … a place where the grass was green and the air was sweet, a place where the stars danced in the moonlight just to see me smile. A place that bad men took away from our family, but now my dreams have given it back to me."

The next day, Yohawni imagined that she and her mother went back to the special place her mother had told her about. It was even more beautiful than her mother described and more beautiful than Yohawni could have ever imagined.

There was a colorful garden and a beach with deep blue, unending water. There were big hills, giant rocks, and a sea of green grass. In the midst of it all was a large home with a beautiful backyard … a backyard just for Yohawni.

STOP Ask the children to draw a picture of this special place.

Yohawni climbed the big hills. She stood on the giant rocks and rolled in the sea of grass. At night, the stars danced in the moonlight just to see Yohawni smile.

Yohawni loved her new home and she loved her beautiful backyard. She was thankful for all that she could see.

Yohawni was very happy. But she never forgot the other children. So she imagined they, too, were playing in her beautiful backyard. They laughed and danced.

Yohawni knew the children's faces. She remembered their voices. Yohawni was pleased that the children were in her backyard and that they were happy.

When the day was done, Yohawni sent her cloud away to rest above the balcony of Apartment 2A for the next child who dreamed of magnificent castles, beautiful gardens, sunny beaches … and of having her very own backyard.

Yohawni smiled peacefully as her special cloud drifted away. For she knew that if she ever needed another soft white cloud or a secret place to dream, all she had to do was close her eyes and wish for it.

FINISH the story by asking the children: "What did Yohawni dream of? What do you dream of?"

ADD FRUITS AND SPICES
(Understanding Emotions)

Ingredients:

Master Chef:
- ✕ No materials required

Student Chefs:
- ☐ Copy of *My Perfect Neighborhood* (page 207)
- ☐ Pencil
- ☐ Crayons

Preparation:

Reproduce *My Perfect Neighborhood* for each child.

Activity:

Distribute *My Perfect Neighborhood,* crayons, and a pencil to each child. Then say:

Pretend you have the power to put whatever you wish in your neighborhood. Then look at the list of things on your activity sheet. Circle those things that you would like to put in your neighborhood. When you have finished, turn your paper over and draw a picture of your perfect neighborhood. When everyone has finished, you may share your drawings.

MY PERFECT NEIGHBORHOOD

Circle the things you would like to put in your neighborhood.

A park

A playground

Pretty flowers

Junk cars and old tires

Lots of trash

A swimming pool

Unsafe old buildings

People who obey the law

People with loud, rude voices

Nicely mowed lawns

Overflowing dumpsters

A movie theater

Broken windows

Now turn your paper over and draw a picture
of your *Perfect Neighborhood.*

GUIDANCE FOR THE GOURMET © 2006 MAR∗CO PRODUCTS, INC. 1-800-448-2197   **207**

REMOVE THE TOUGH STEMS
(Information And Facts)

Ingredients:

Master Chef:
✗ No materials required

Student Chefs:
☐ Drawing paper
☐ Pencil
☐ Crayons

Preparation:

None required.

Activity:

Distribute a piece of drawing paper, crayons, and a pencil to each child. Then say:

> Yohawni went to her balcony and escaped from her real world by imagining that she had a beautiful garden. When you want to escape, where do you go to feel safe? Draw a picture of that place.

When the children have finished, have them share their pictures.

DRIZZLE WITH DRESSING
(Coping Strategies)

Ingredients:

Master Chef:
- ✗ No materials required

Student Chefs:
- ☐ Copy of *Do You Know What To Do?* (page 208)
- ☐ Pencil

Preparation:

Reproduce *Do You Know What To Do?* for each child.

Activity:

Distribute *Do You Know What To Do?* and a pencil to each child. Then say:

It is important to know what to do when certain things or feelings happen to you. Look at your activity sheet and write what you would do if you had any of these feelings or had any of these things happen near you. When you have finished, we will discuss your answers.

DO YOU KNOW WHAT TO DO?

Complete each sentence below by telling what you would do in each situation.

If you were frightened, _____

_____ .

If you felt unsafe, _____

_____ .

If you got lonely, _____

_____ .

If your neighbors were too loud, _____

_____ .

If you heard sirens, _____

_____ .

In case of an emergency, _____

_____ .

If someone tried to harm you, _____

_____ .

208

GUIDANCE FOR THE GOURMET © 2006 MAR★CO PRODUCTS, INC. 1-800-448-2197

TOSS AND EAT
(Therapeutic Activities)

Ingredients:

Master Chef:
- ☐ Sample *My Dream Home*
- ☐ Various colors of construction paper
- ☐ Newspapers
- ☐ Various colors of paint
- ☐ Paintbrushes
- ☐ Tables

Student Chefs:
- ☐ Shoe box
- ☐ Blue and green construction paper
- ☐ Scissors
- ☐ Empty toilet paper roll
- ☐ Piece of cardboard
- ☐ Glue
- ☐ Crayons or markers
- ☐ Pencil

Preparation:

Make a sample *Dream House* by following the activity directions. Cover a table with newspaper and make a paint station with various colors of paint and paintbrushes. In another place in the room, place various colors of construction paper (other than blue and green) on a table.

Activity:

Distribute a shoe box, cardboard, glue, scissors, pencil, crayons or markers, green and blue construction paper, and empty toilet paper roll to each child. Then say:

Today, you are going to create your *Dream House*. The shoe box will be your house, and you can make it and your yard exactly the way you would like. First, come to the paint table and paint your house any color you wish. When you have finished, put it aside to dry and return to your seat.

While you are waiting for your house to dry, think about your yard. Use your toilet paper roll to make a tree for your yard. Do this by drawing four circles onto the green construction paper to make the treetops. Cut out the treetops, making scallops. Then cut four small slits on the sides of the toilet paper roll and slide a scalloped top into each slit.

Make your own personal lake by cutting a lake out of the blue construction paper and gluing it to the cardboard. Be careful not to glue it where your house will be. Now tear the green construction paper into small pieces. Then glue these pieces onto the cardboard for grass.

Your house should be dry now, so draw some windows and a door. You may cut out three sides of the door so it will open. If you wish to cut out the windows, you may do so and get different colors of construction paper to make curtains and glue them to your windows. Place your tree and house on the cardboard.

These are only suggestions. You may add anything you want or leave anything out that you do not want. Use your imagination and have fun!

MY PERFECT NEIGHBORHOOD

Circle the things you would like to put in your neighborhood.

A park

A playground

Pretty flowers

Junk cars and old tires

Lots of trash

A swimming pool

Unsafe old buildings

People who obey the law

People with loud, rude voices

Nicely mowed lawns

Overflowing dumpsters

A movie theater

Broken windows

**Now turn your paper over and draw a picture
of your *Perfect Neighborhood*.**

DO YOU KNOW WHAT TO DO?

Complete each sentence below by telling what you would do in each situation.

If you were frightened, _____

_____ .

If you felt unsafe, _____

_____ .

If you got lonely, _____

_____ .

If your neighbors were too loud, _____

_____ .

If you heard sirens, _____

_____ .

In case of an emergency, _____

_____ .

If someone tried to harm you, _____

_____ .